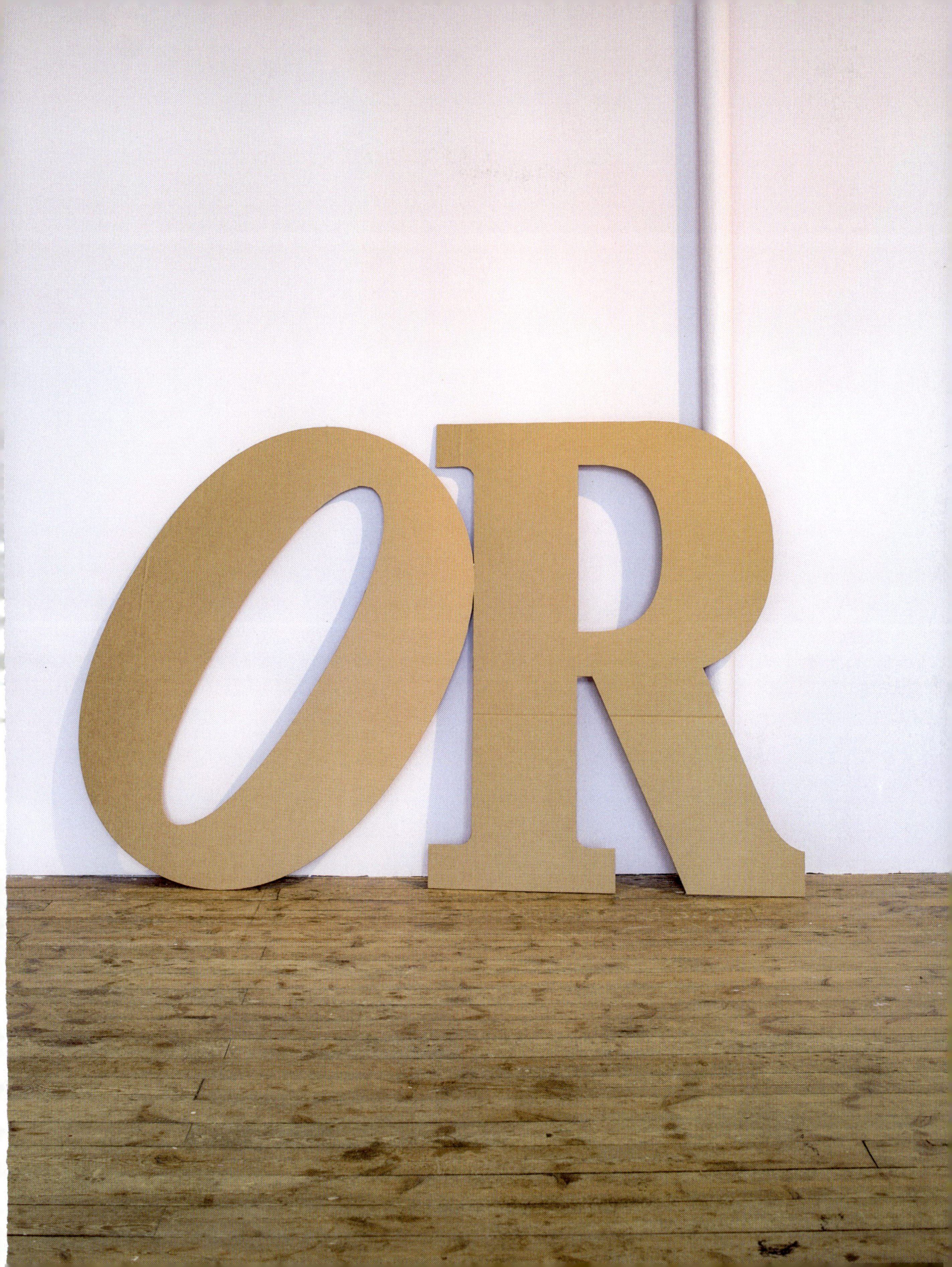
OR

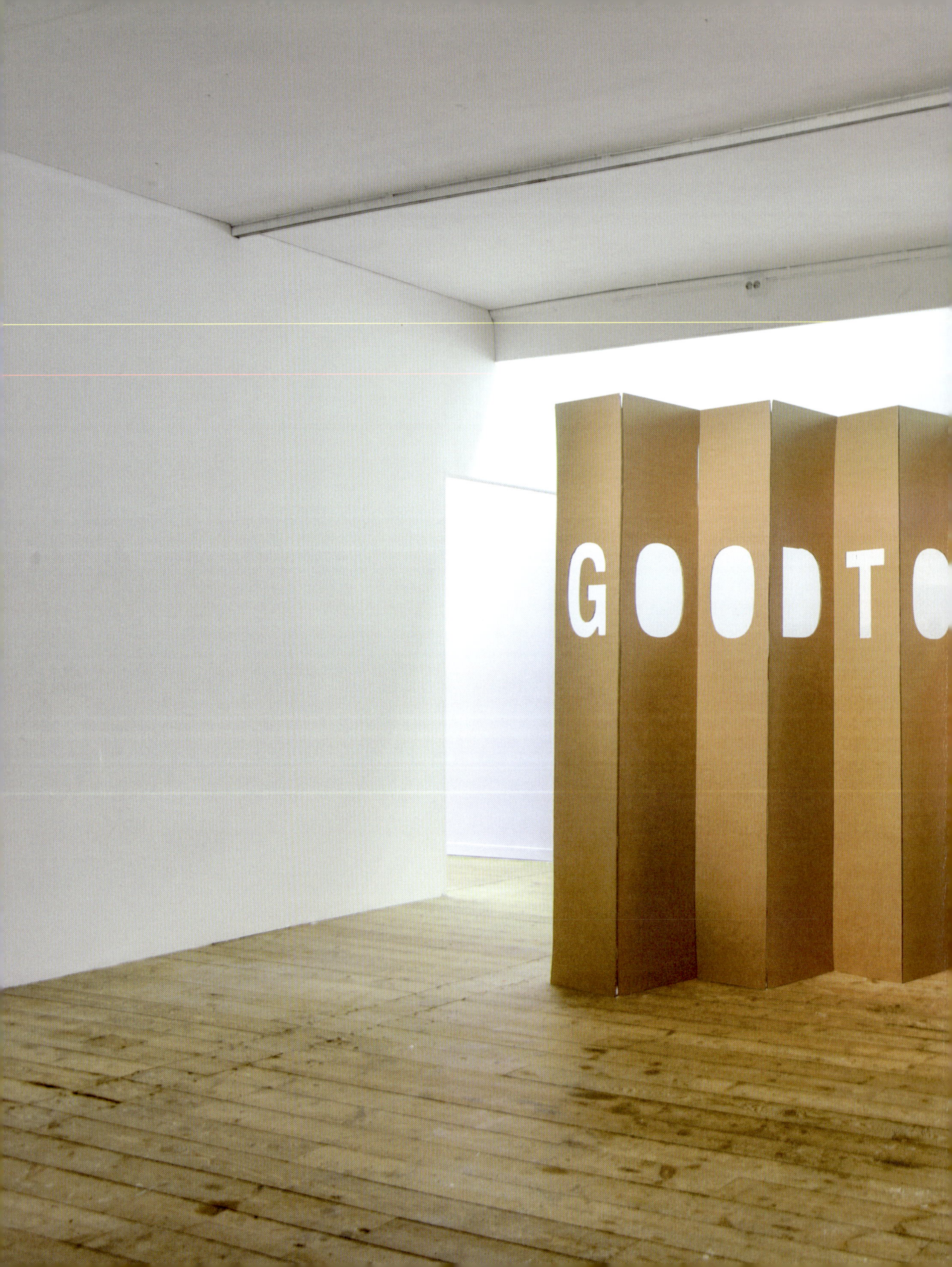
GOODT

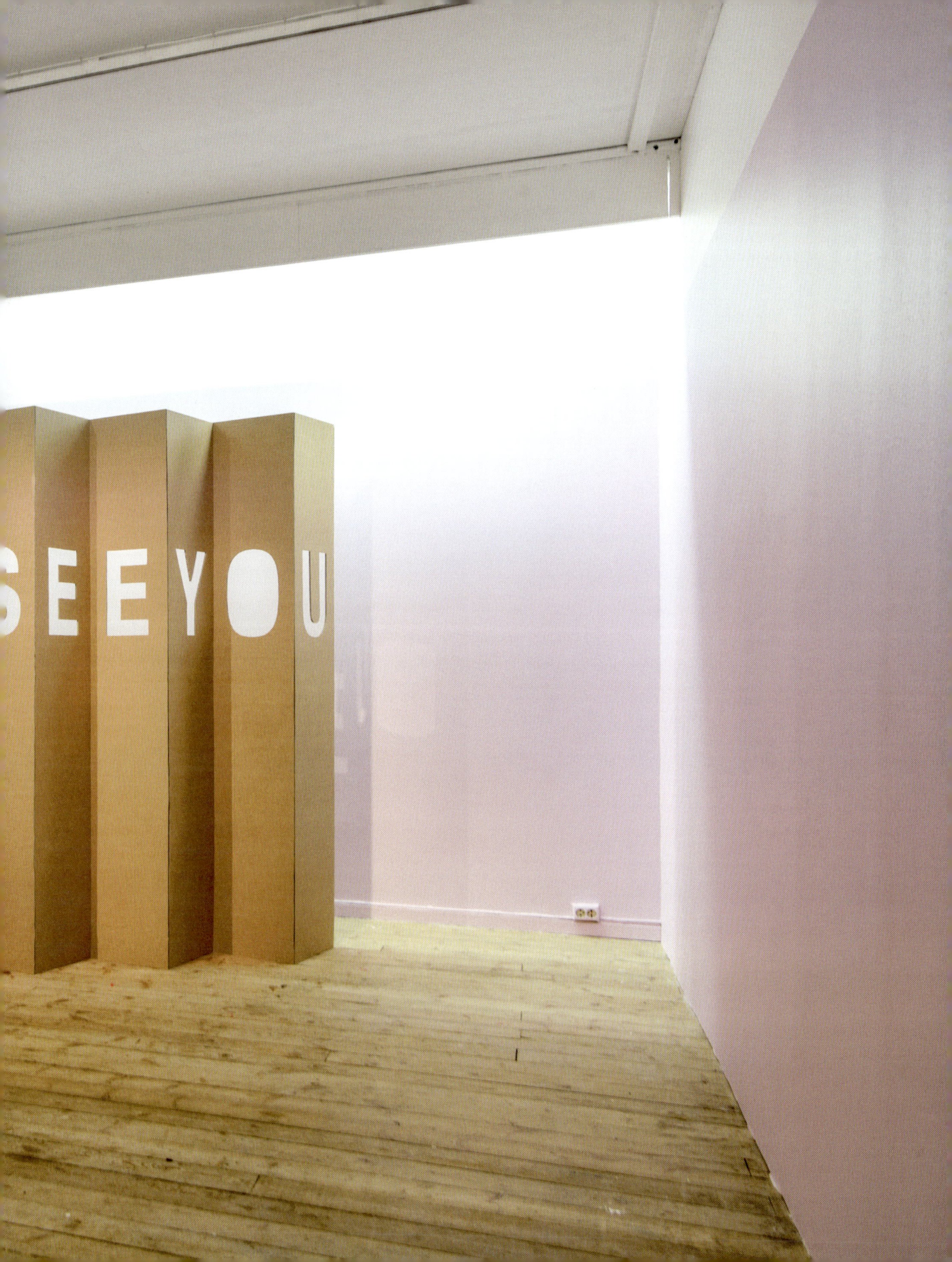
SEEYOU

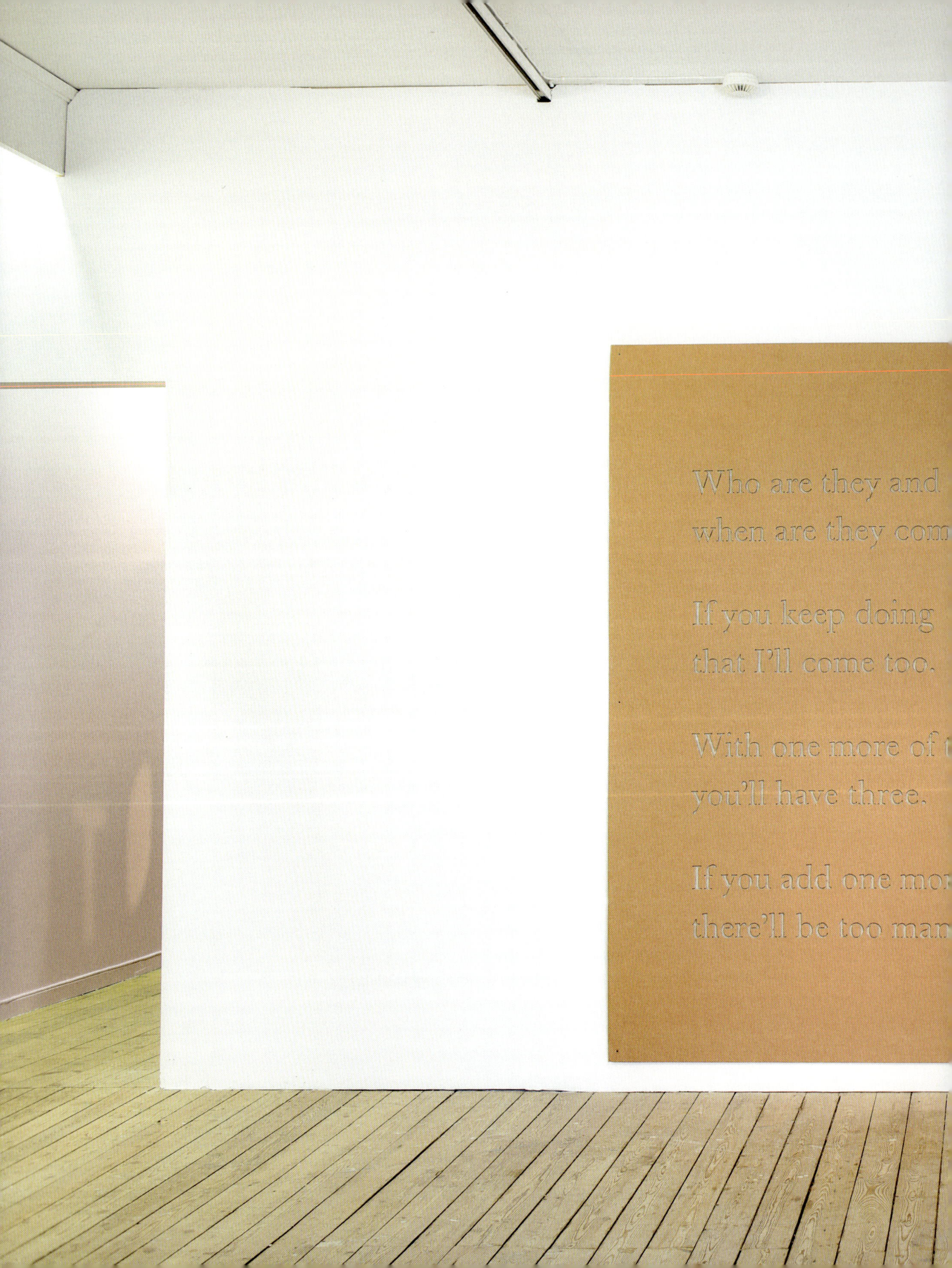
Who are they and
when are they
If you keep doing
that I'll come too.
With one more of
you'll have three.
If you add one
there'll be too

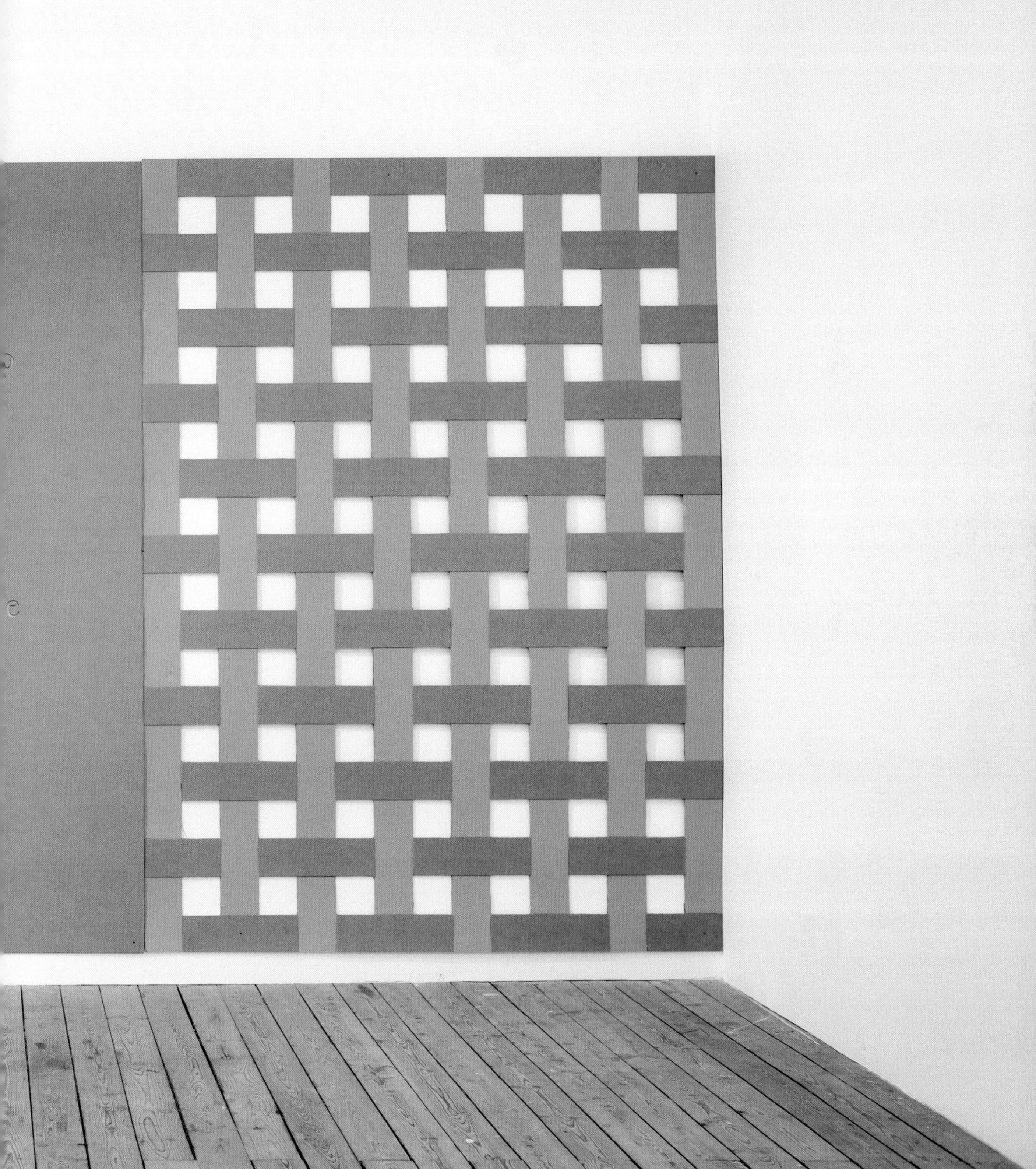

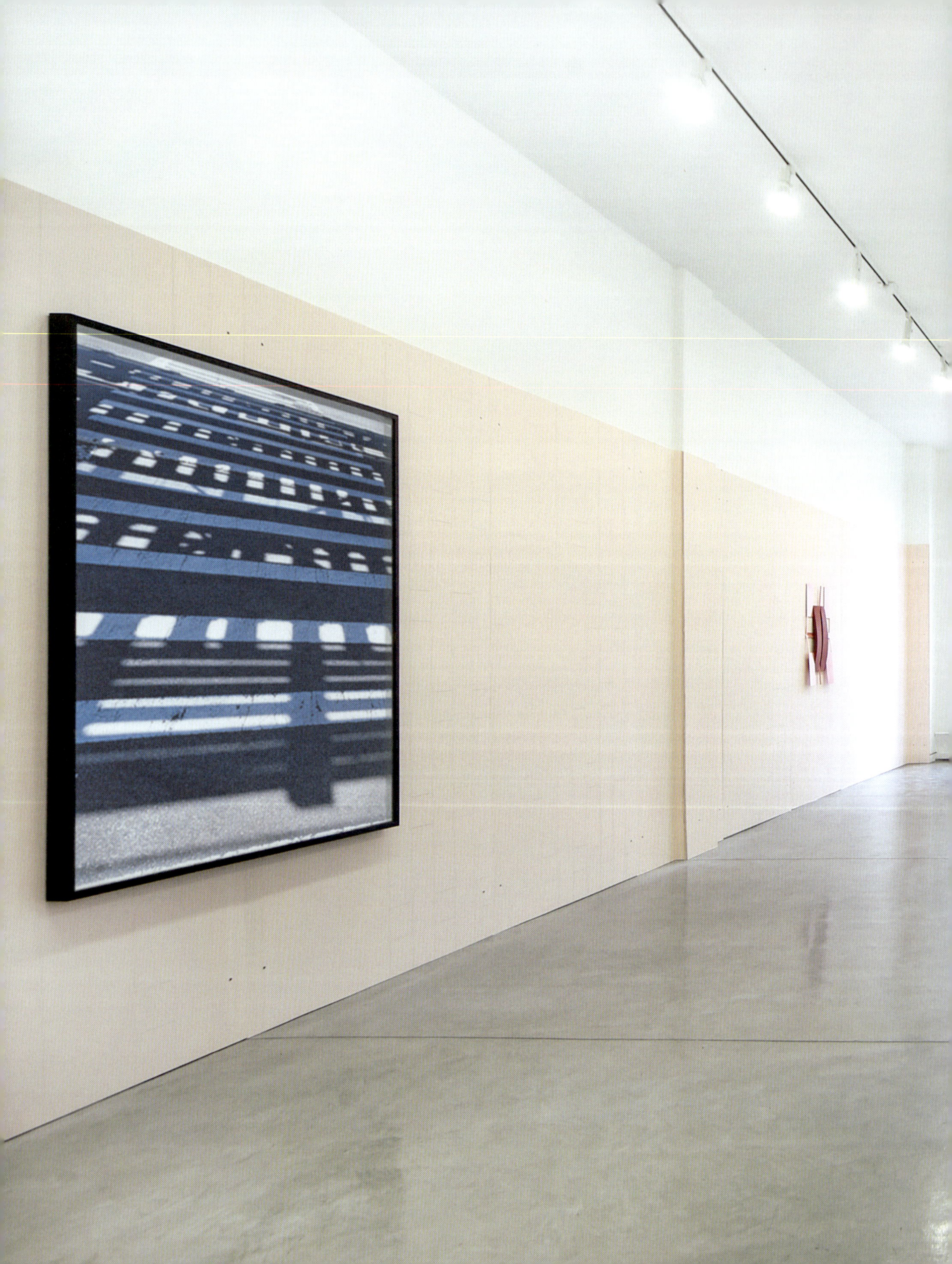

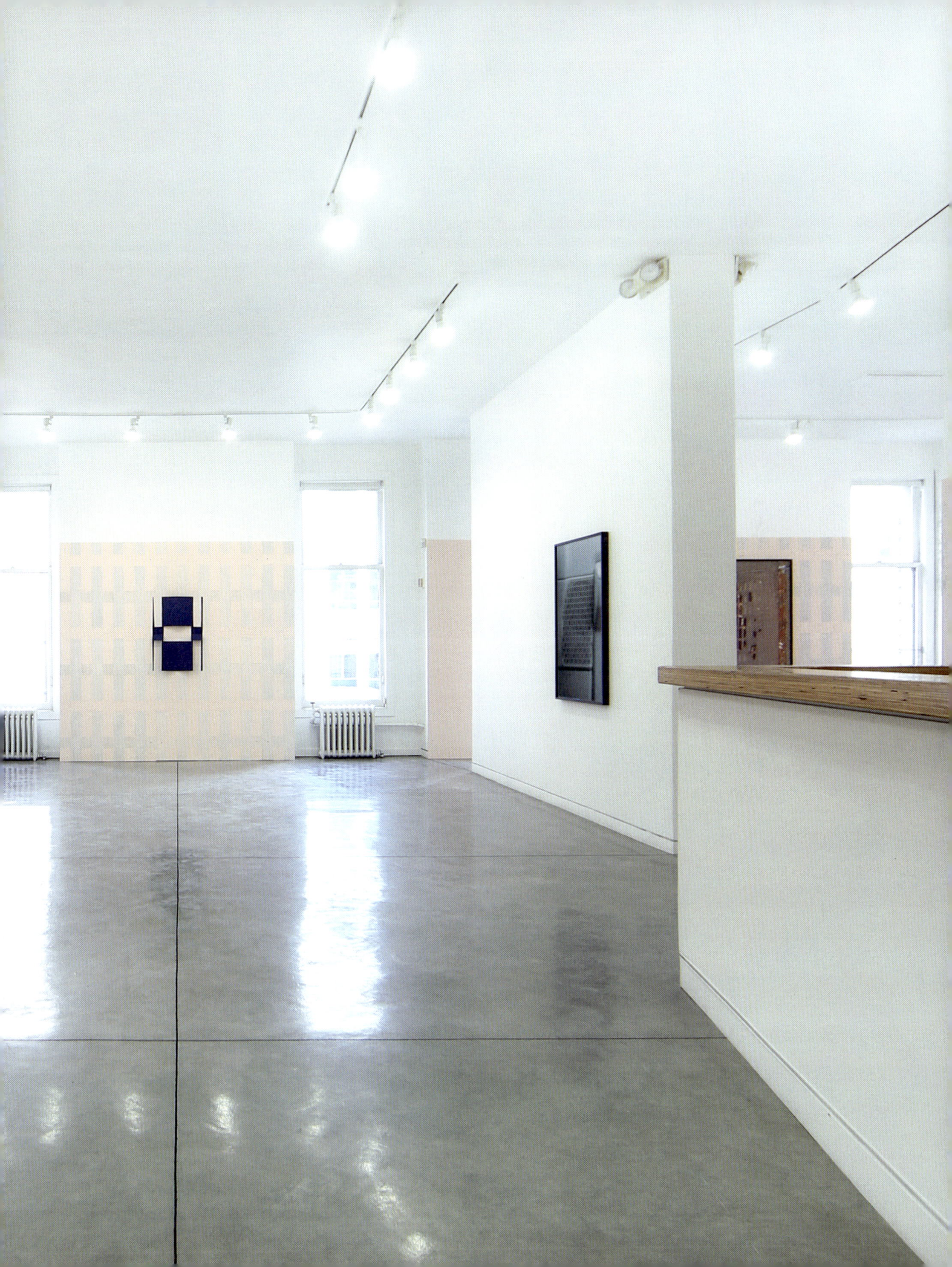

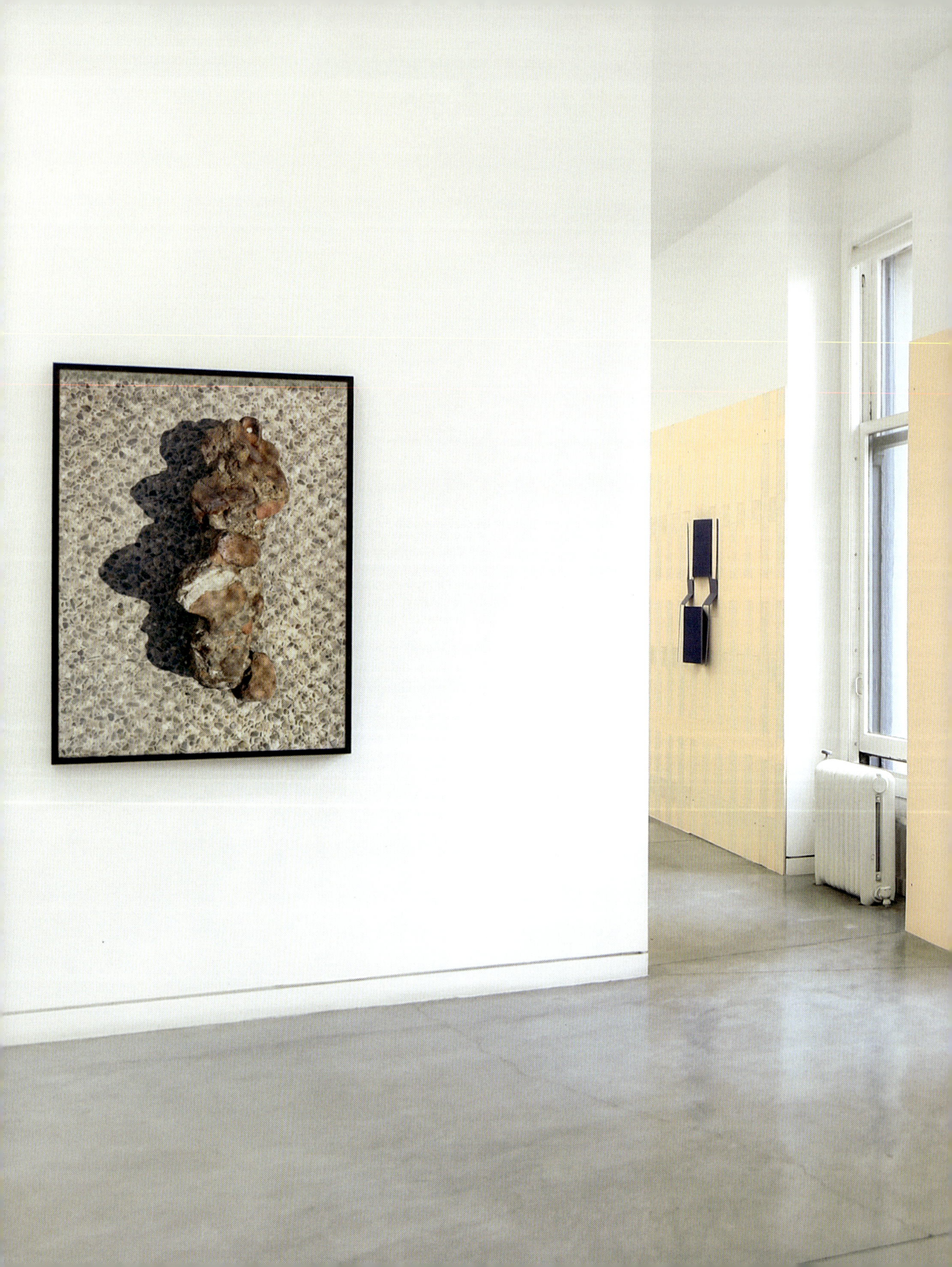

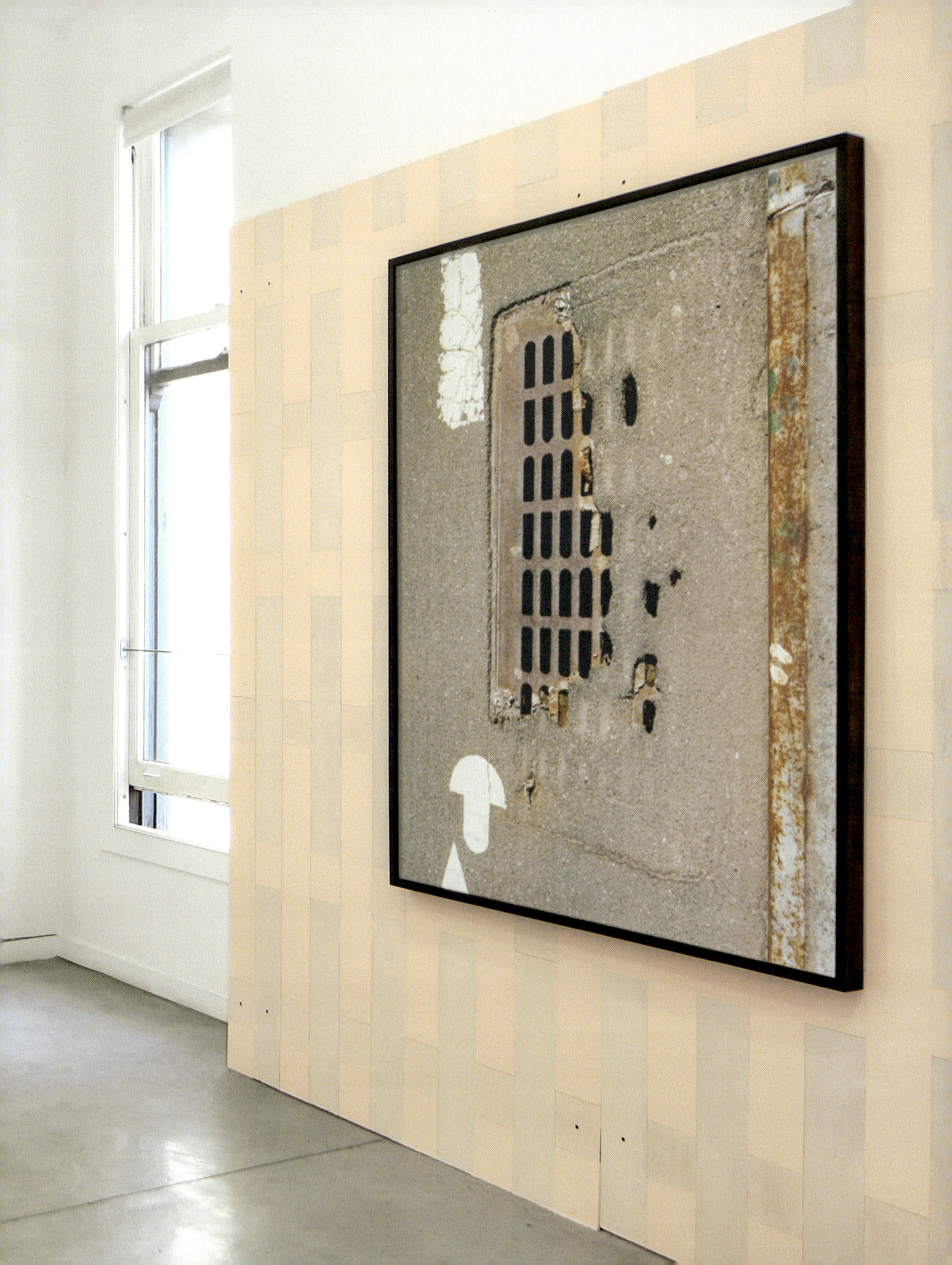

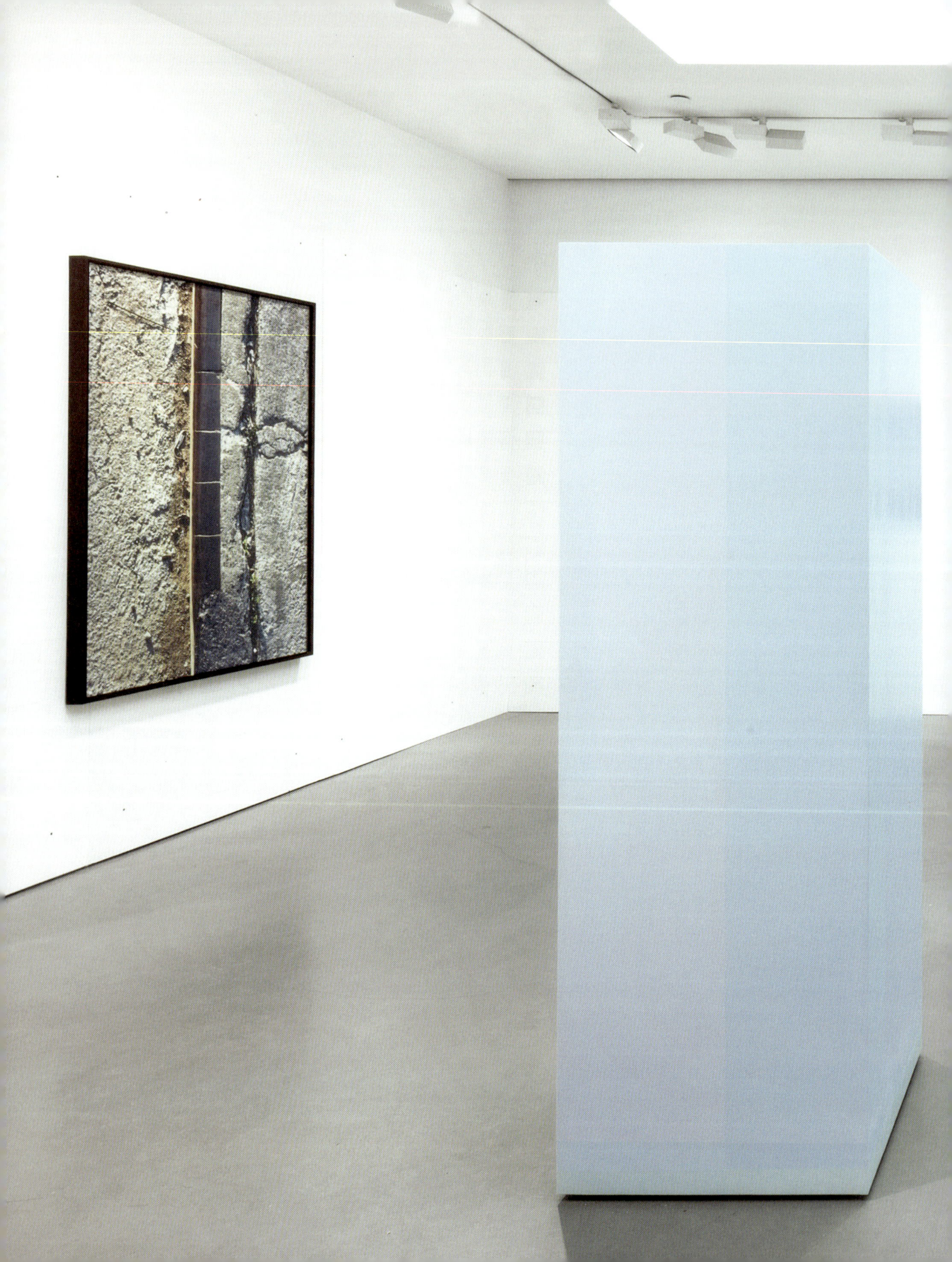

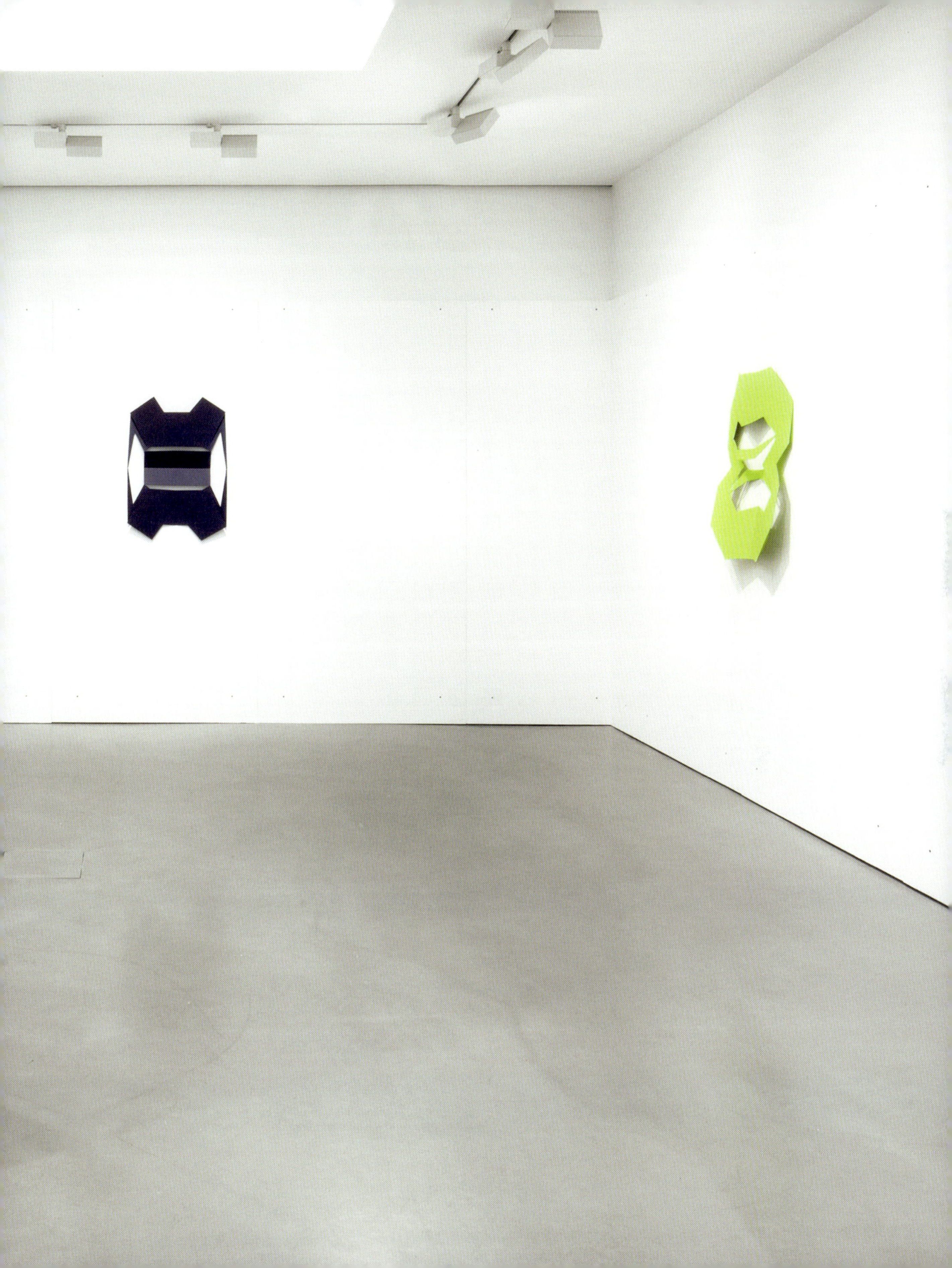

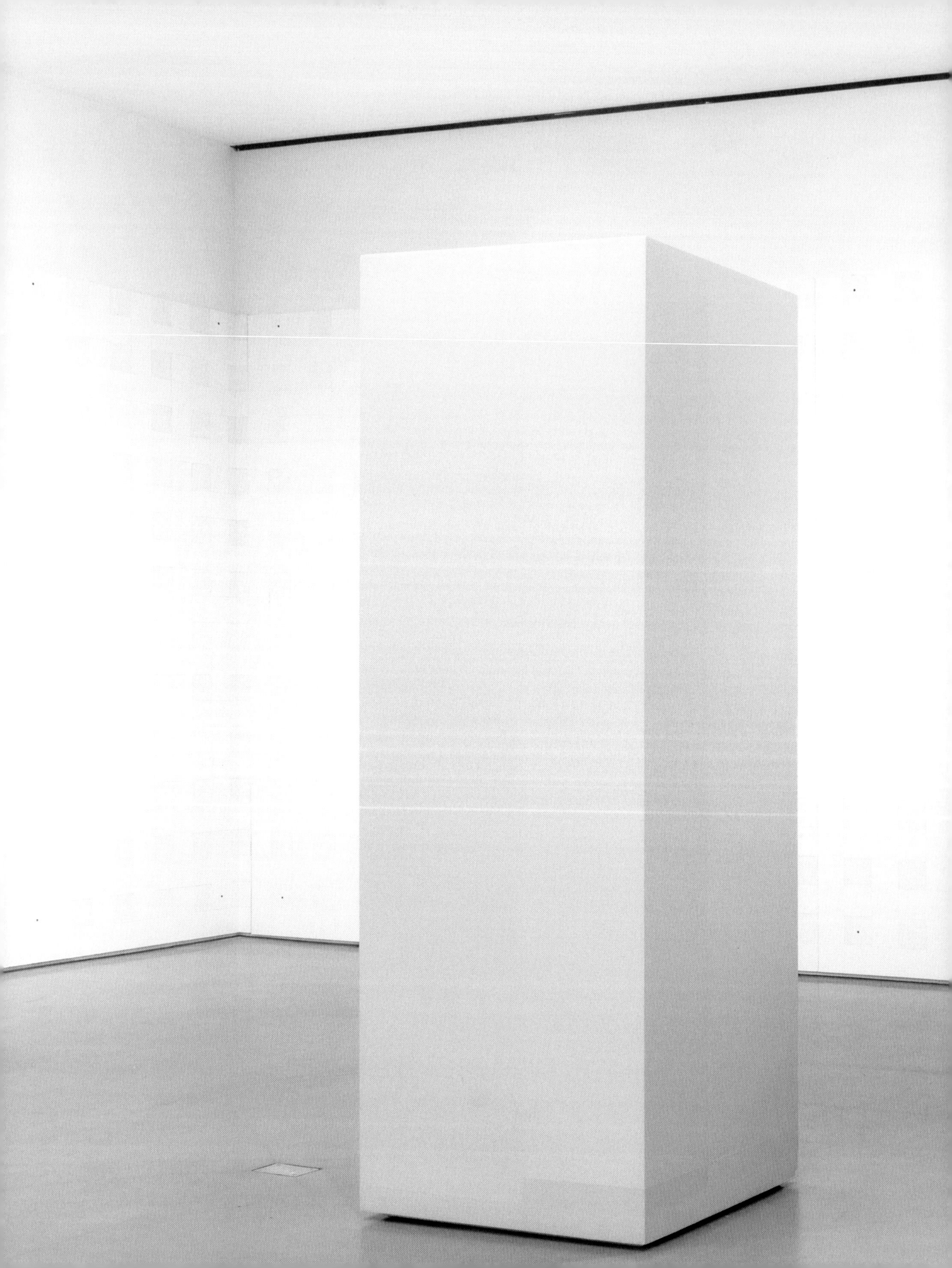

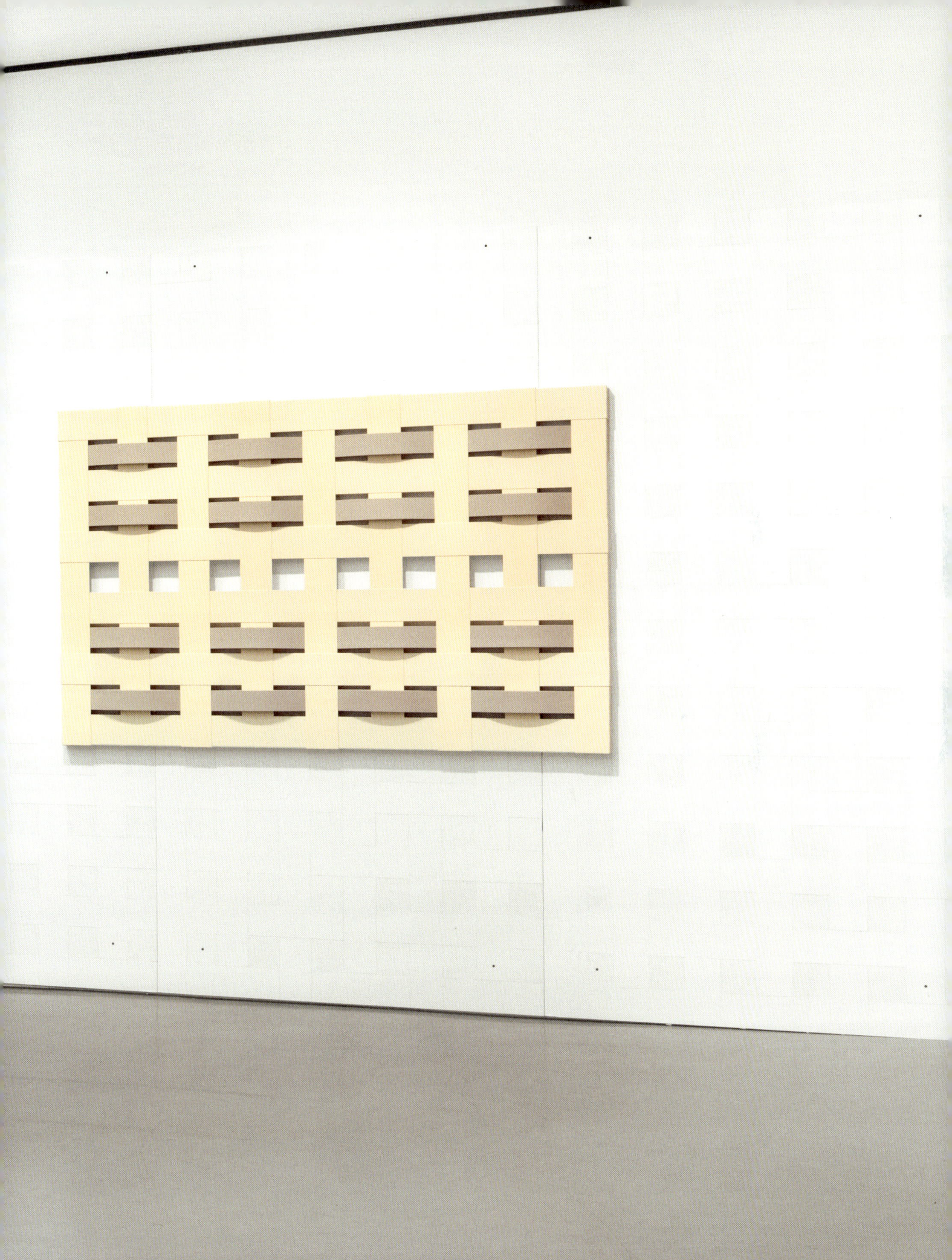

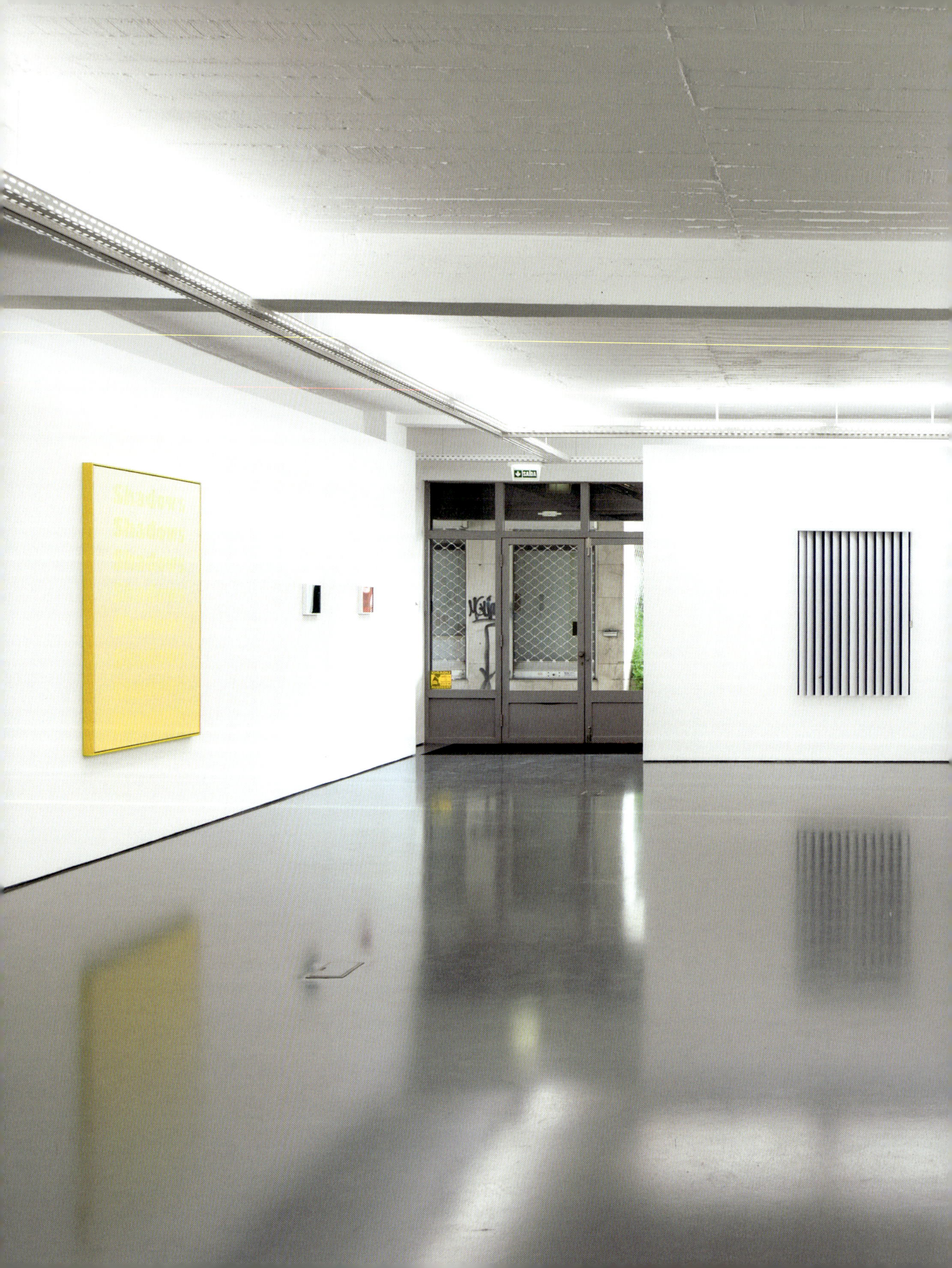

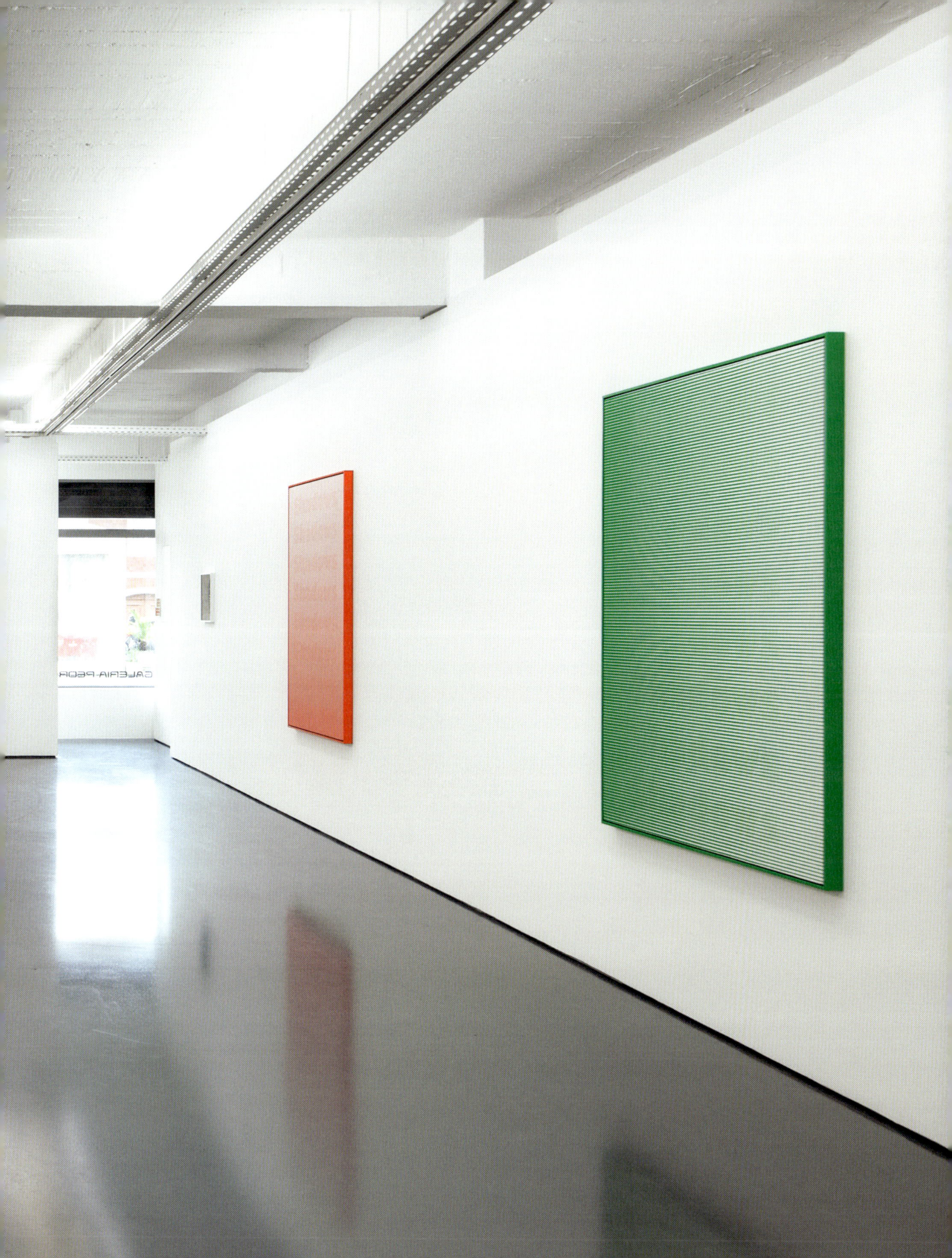

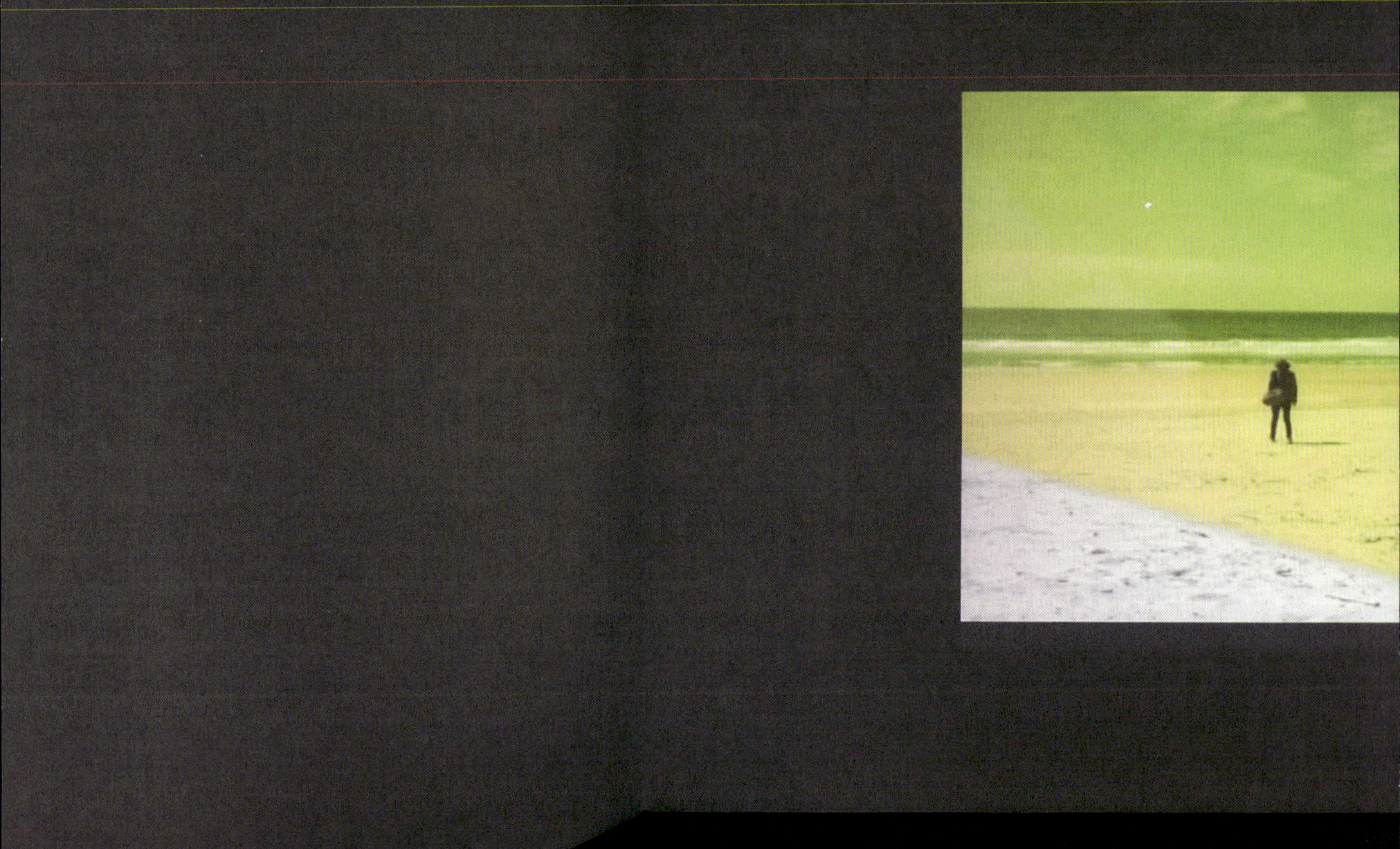

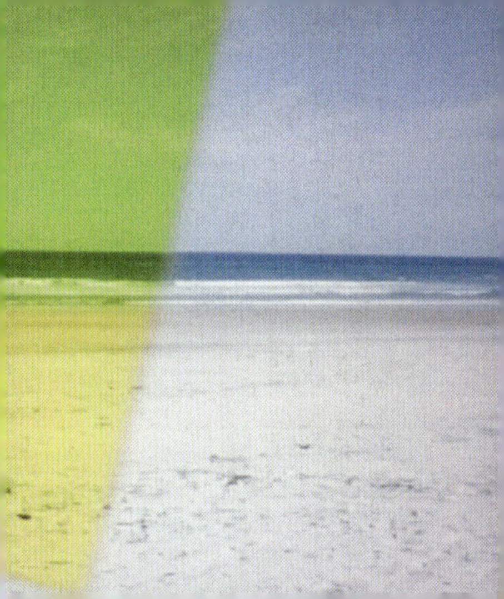

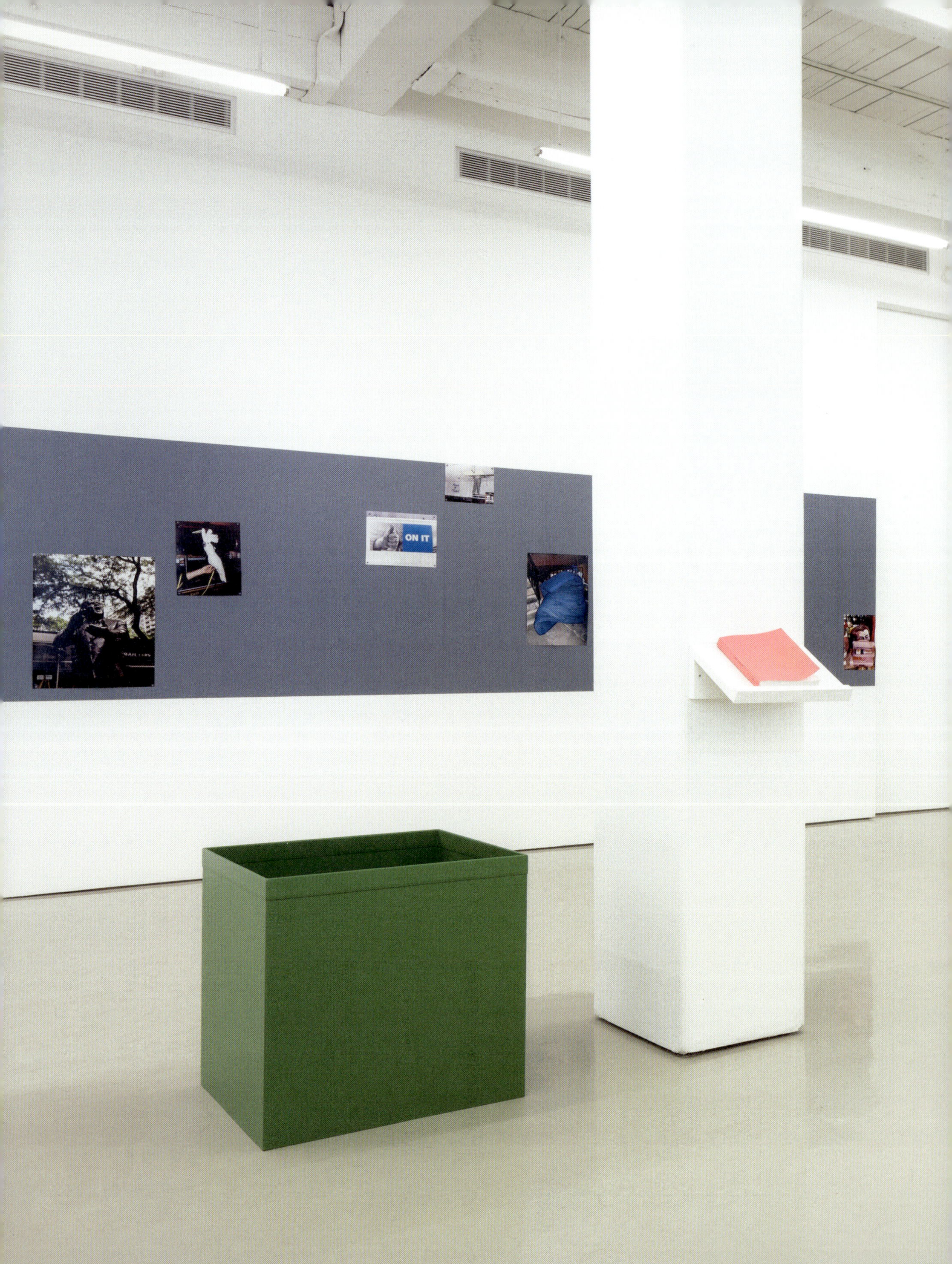
ON IT

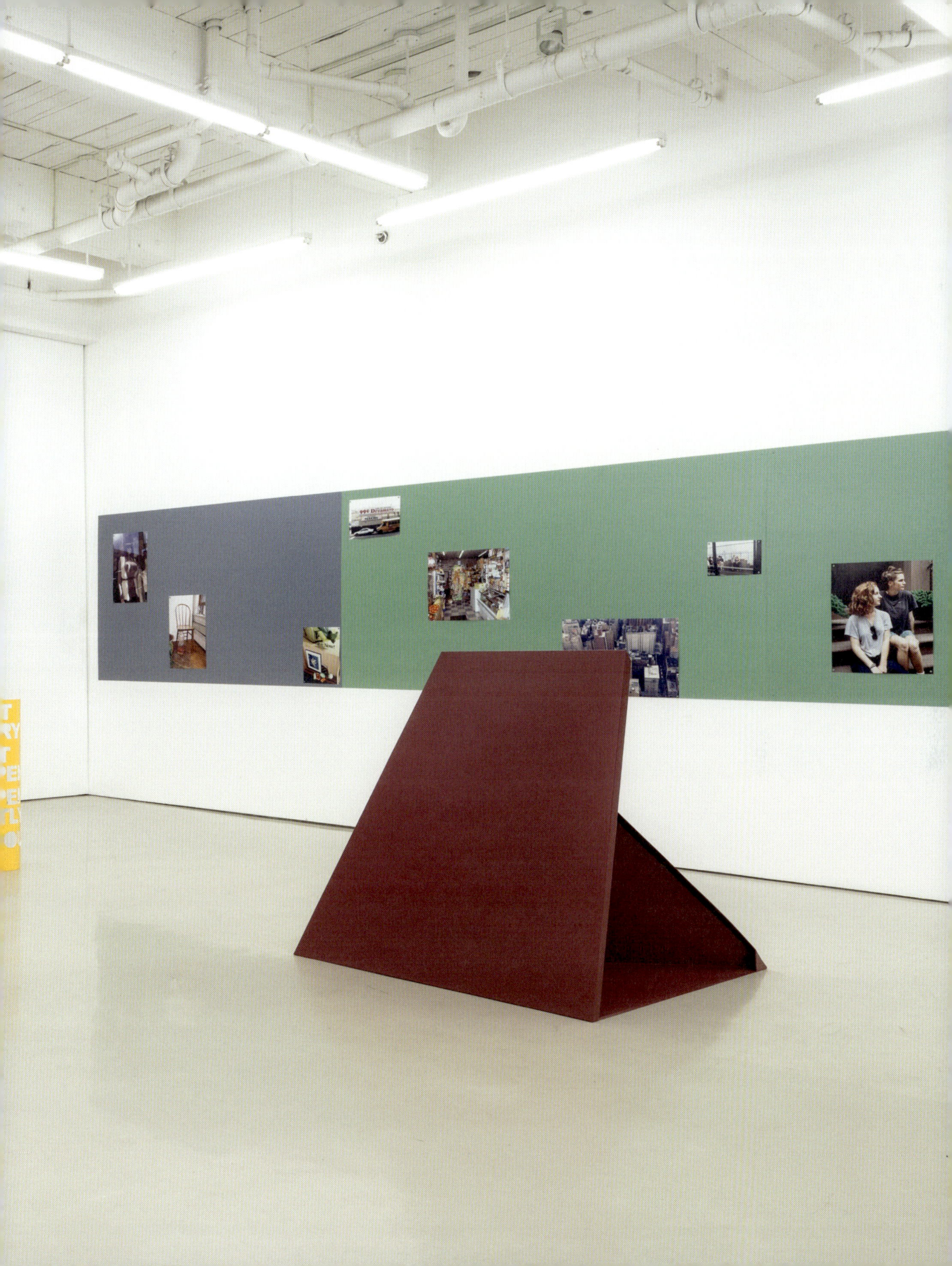

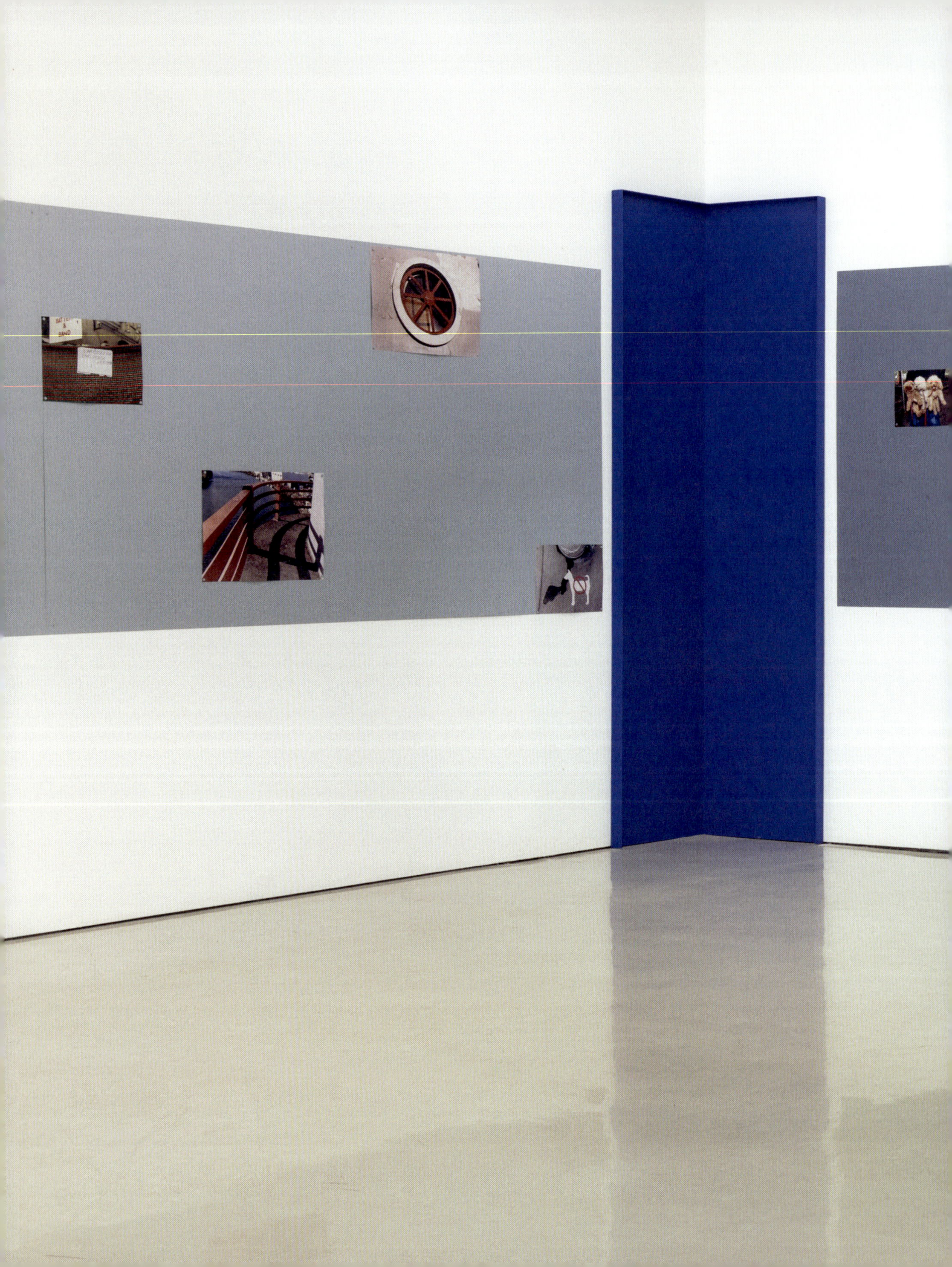

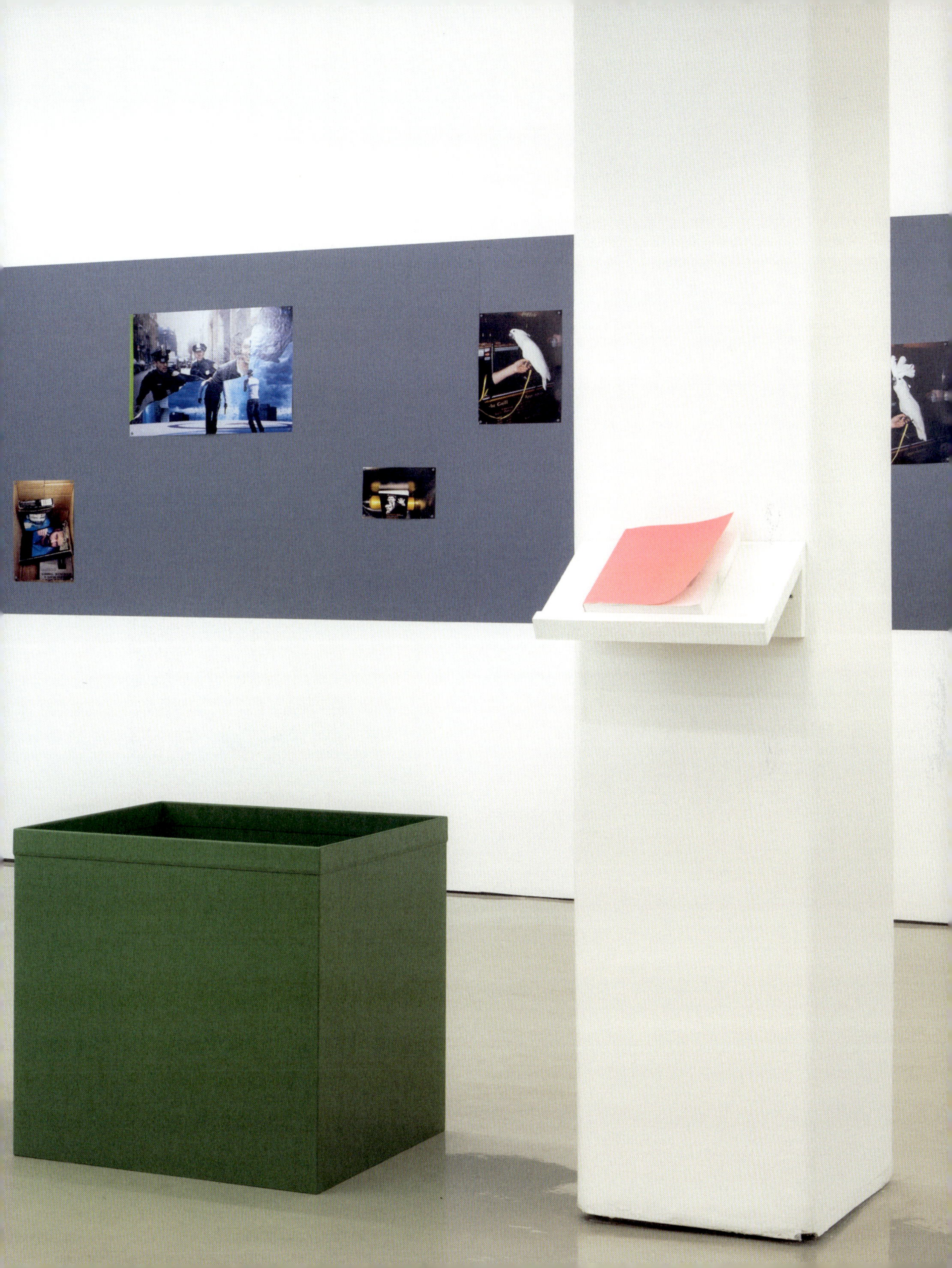

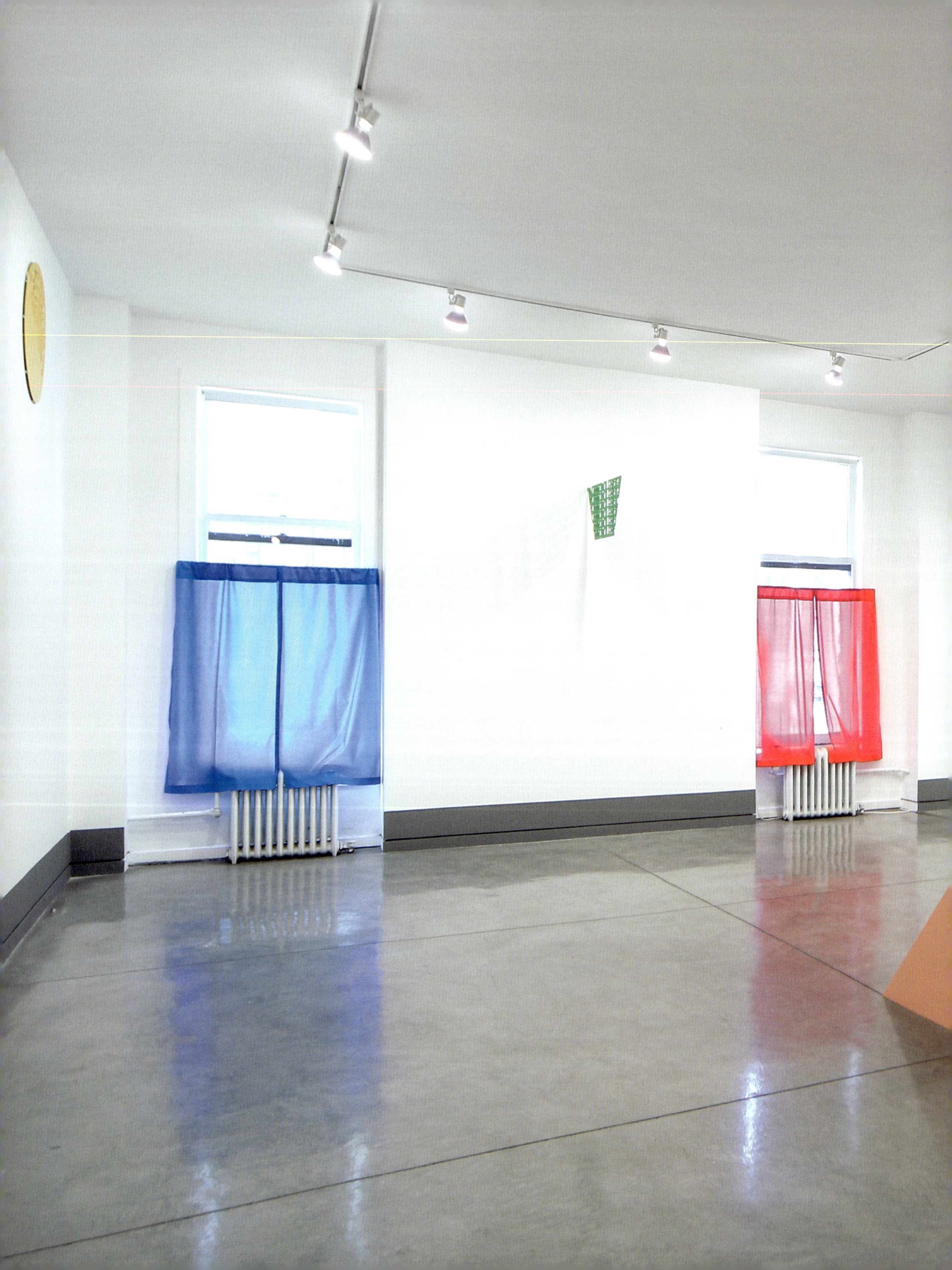

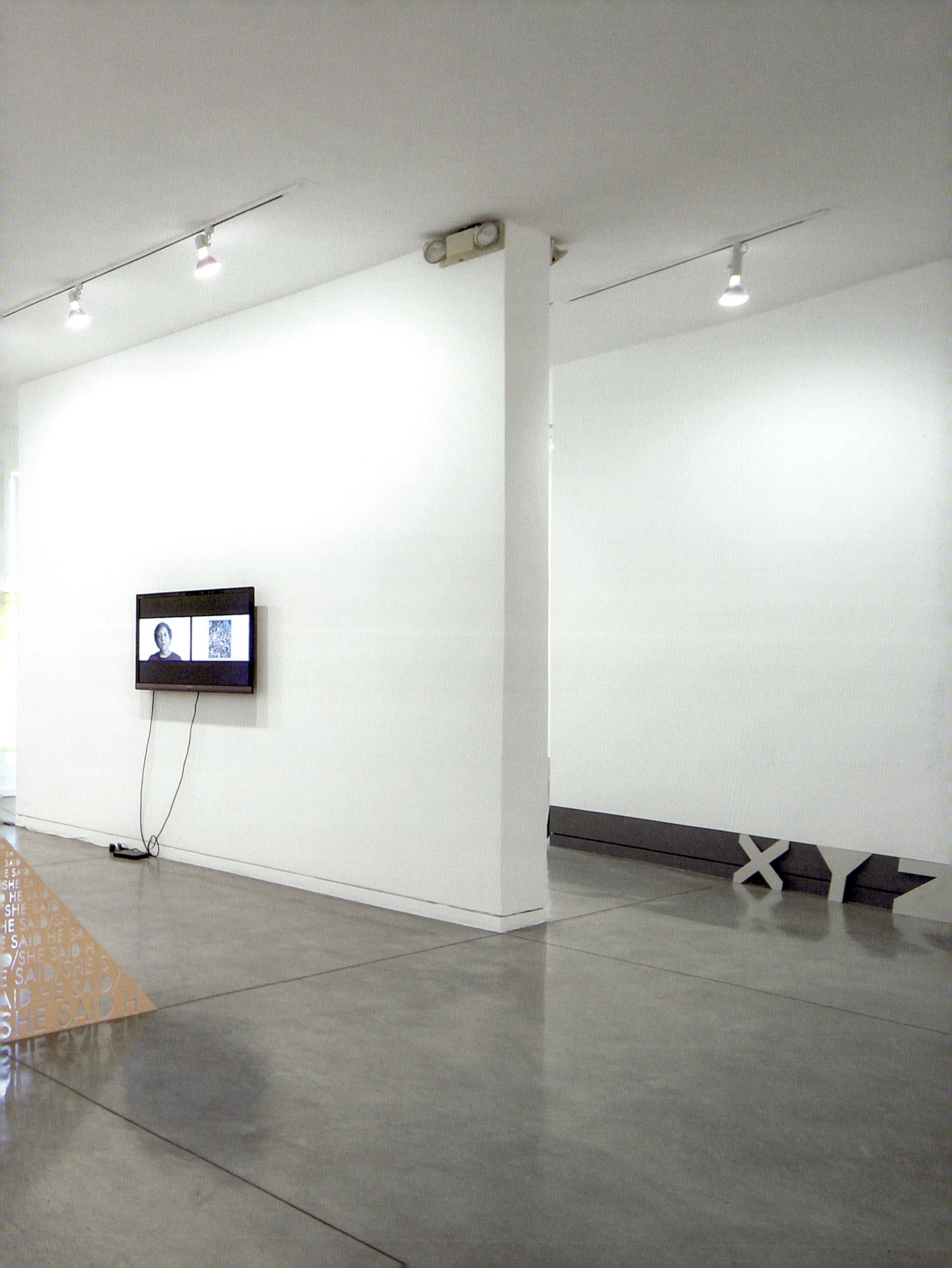
XY

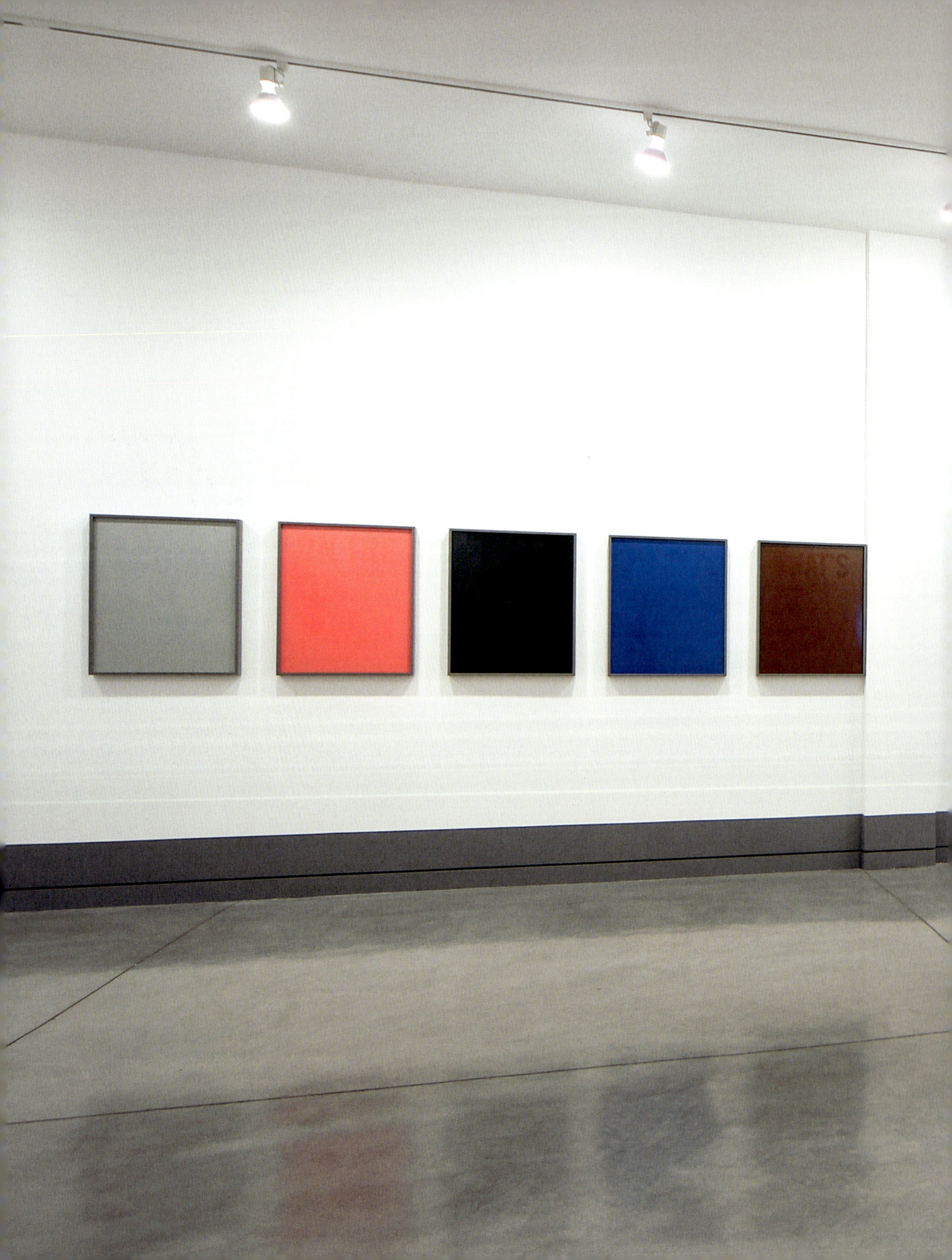

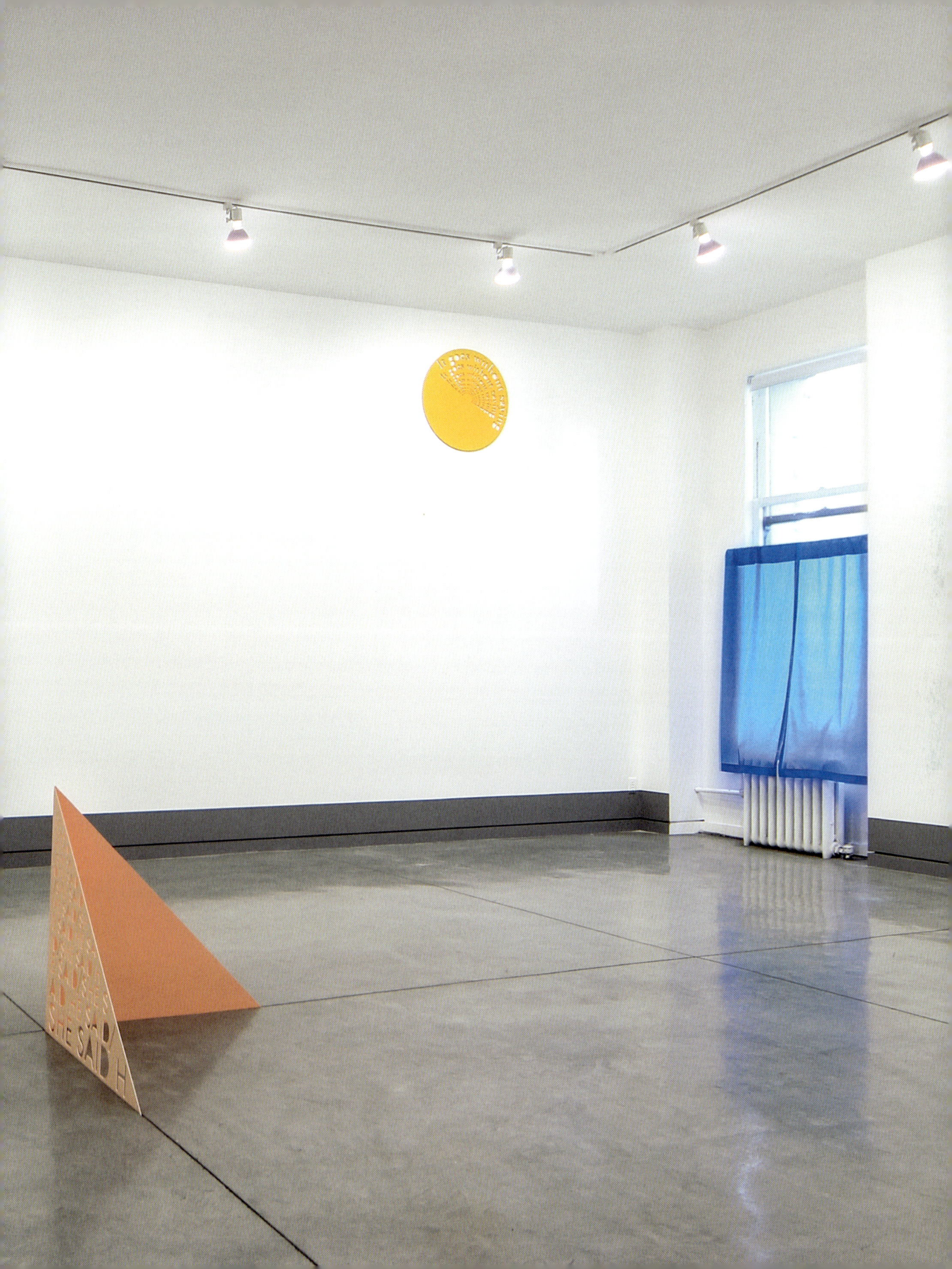
it goes without saying
SHE SAID

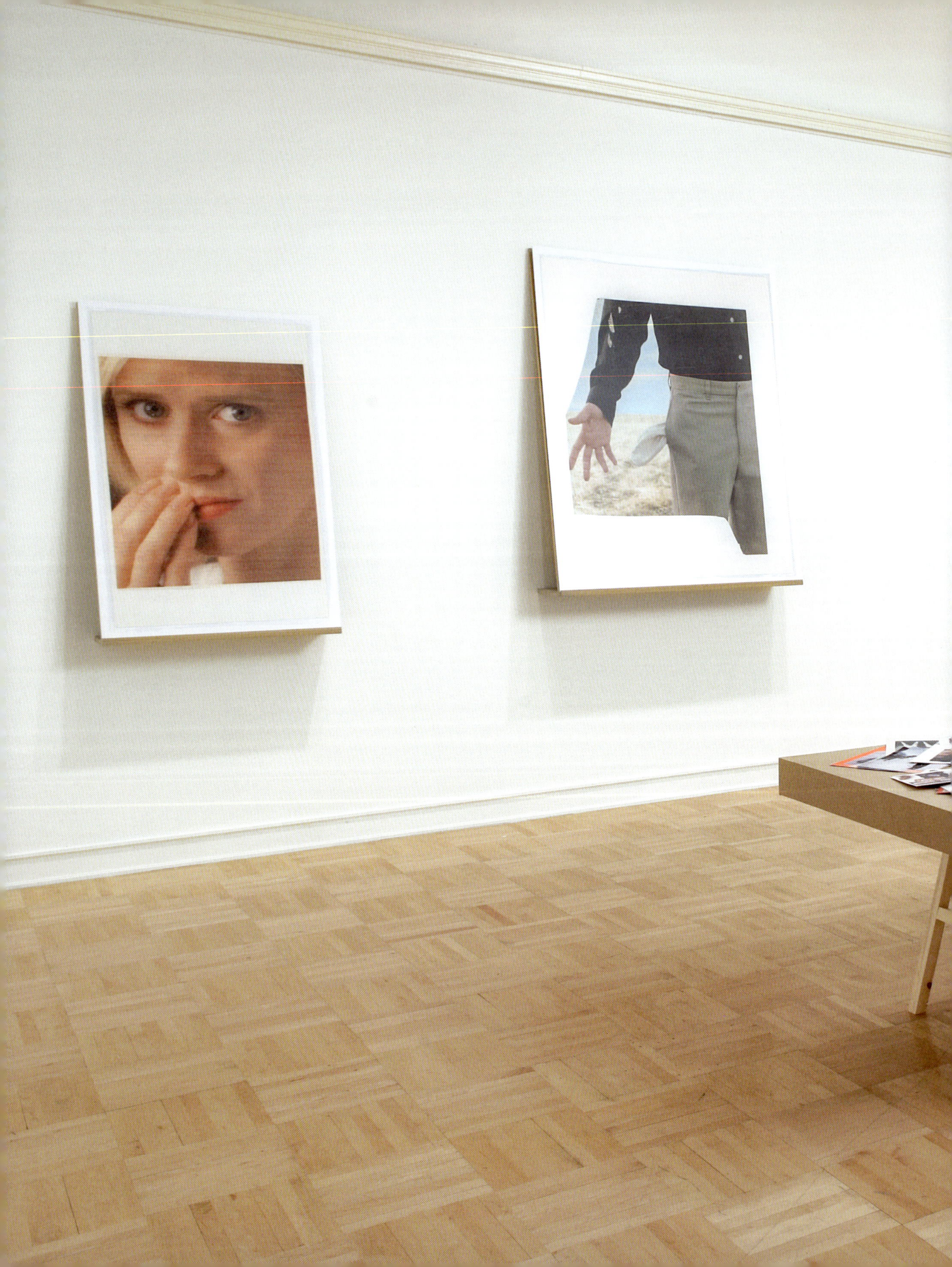

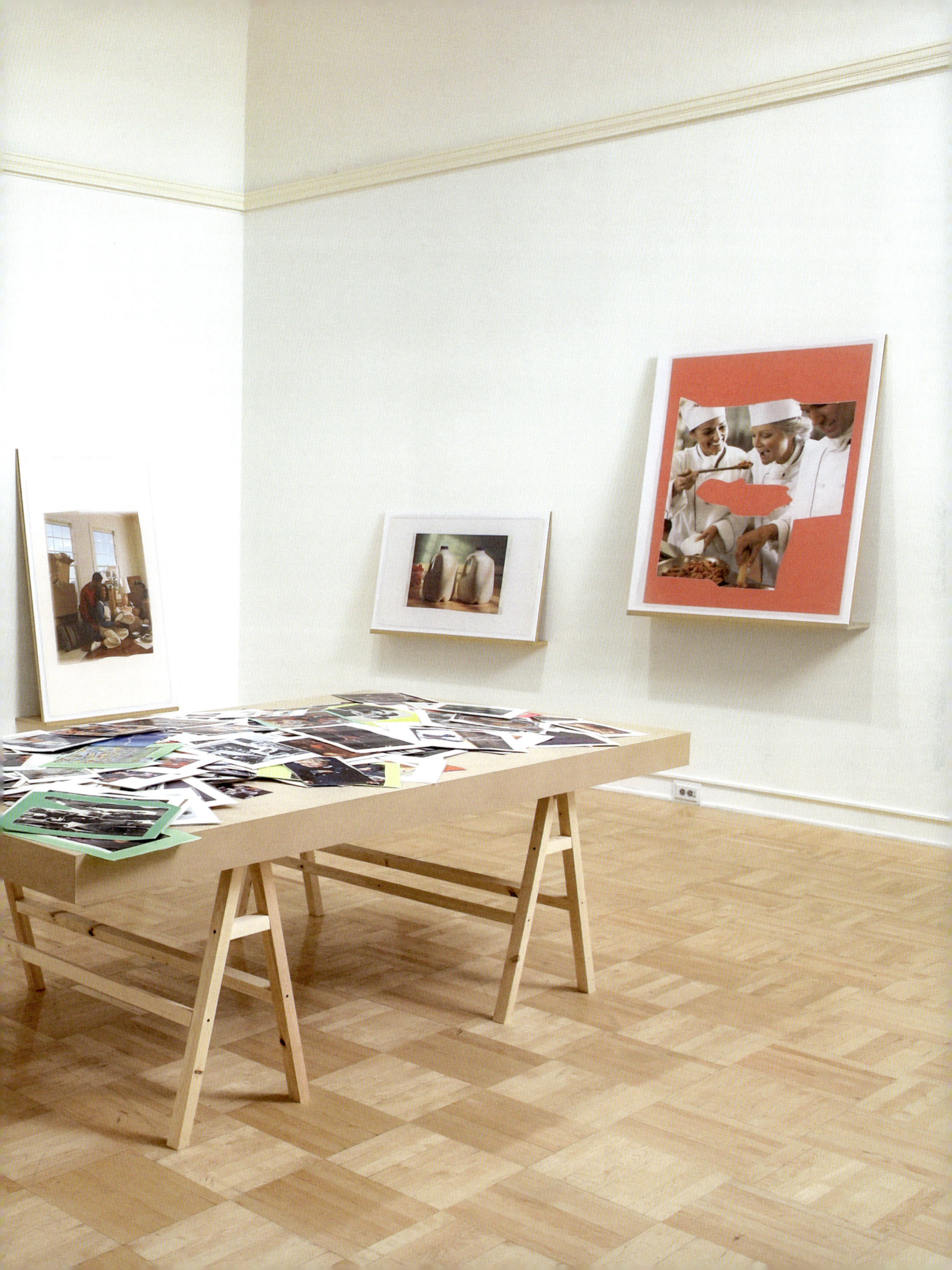

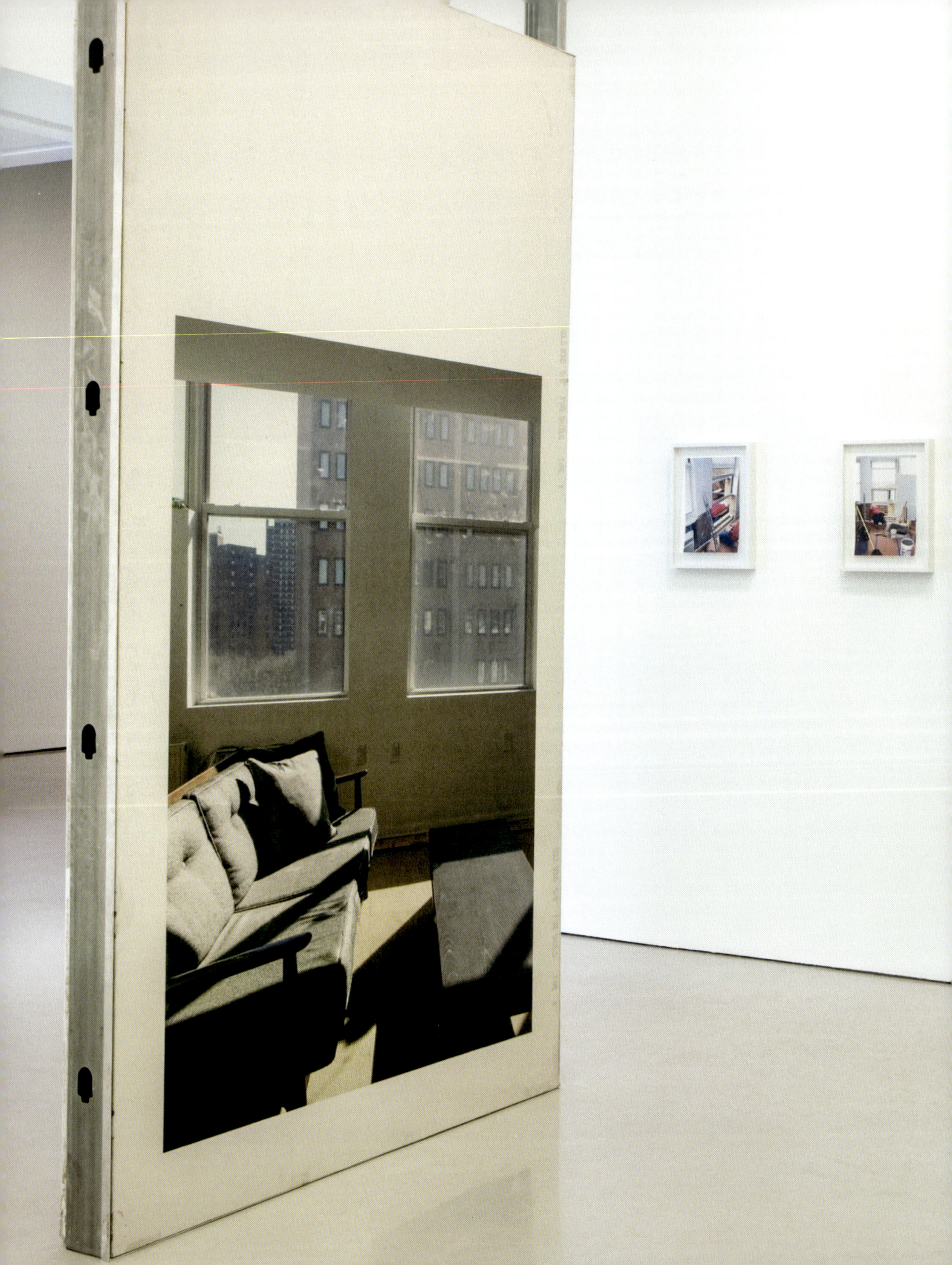

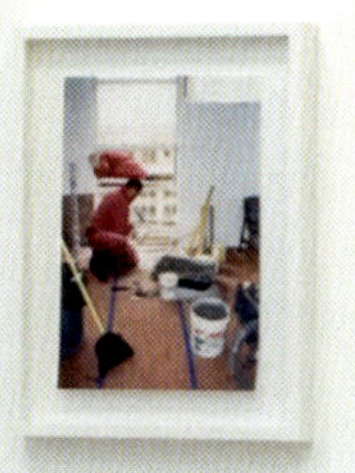
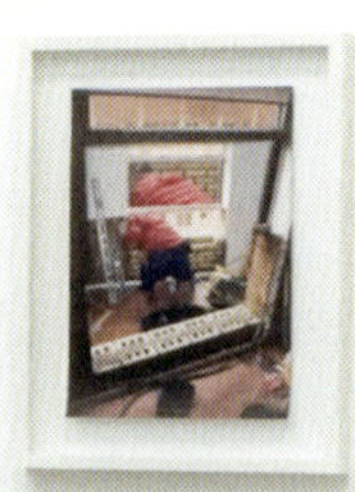
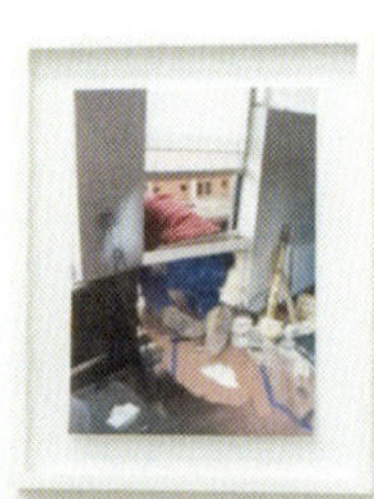
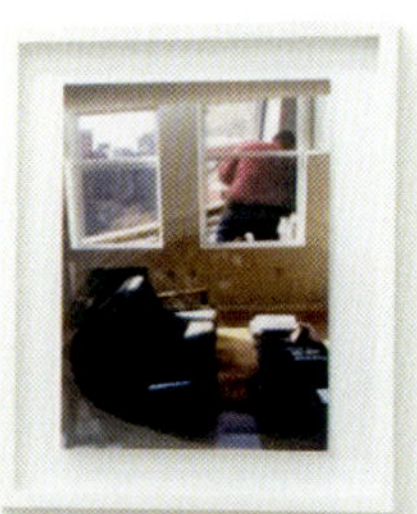

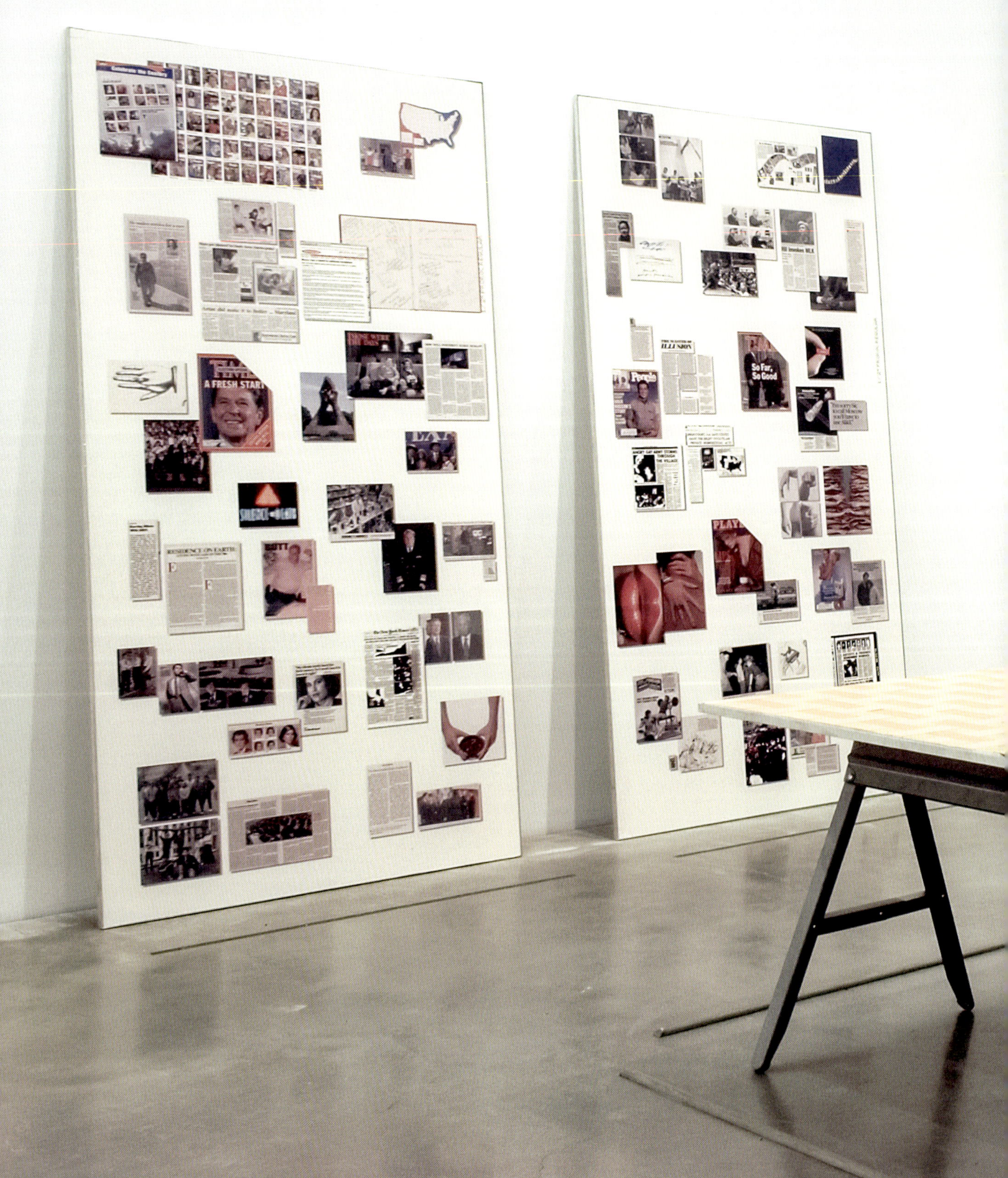

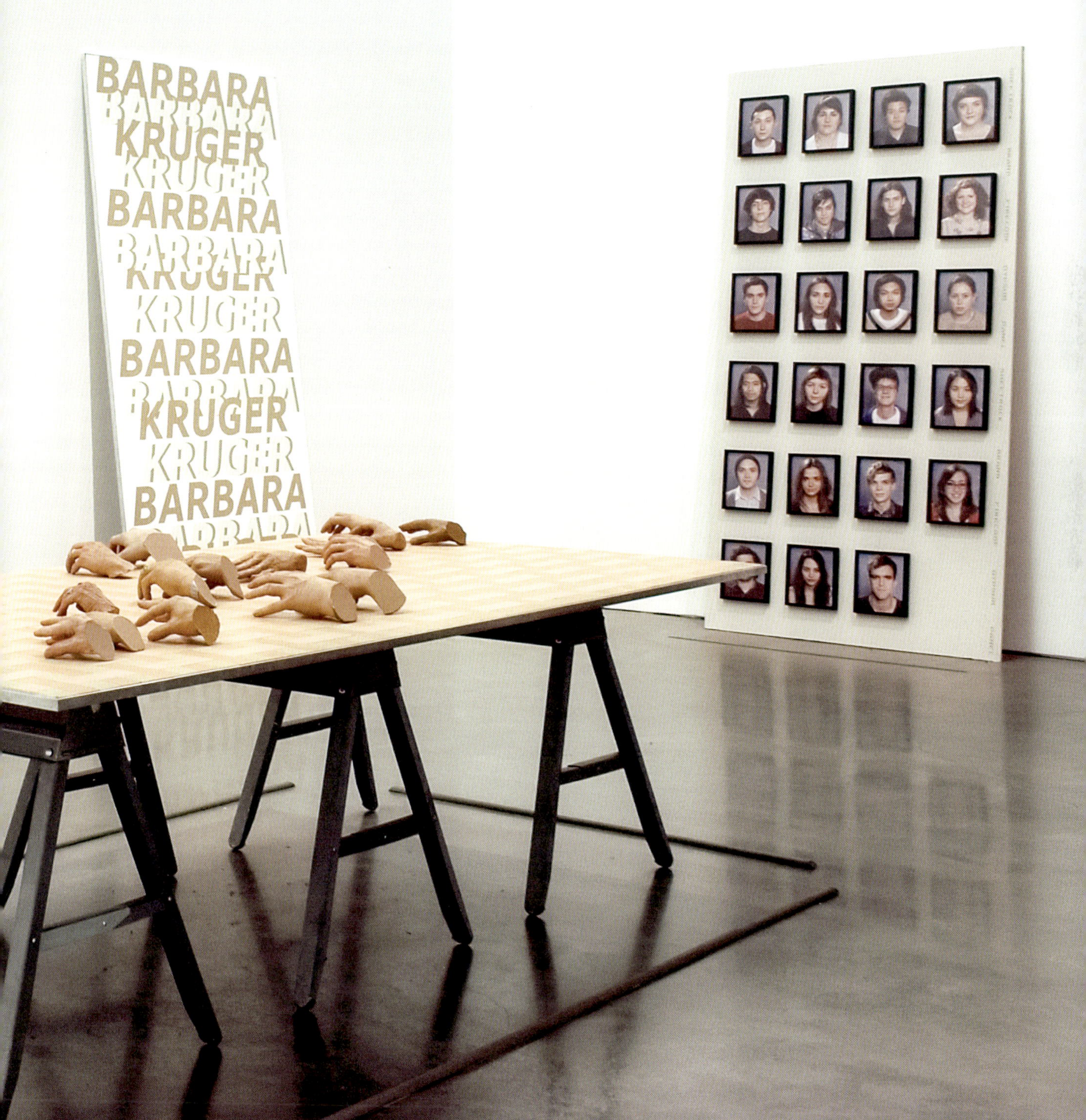
BARBARA
KRUGER
BARBARA
KRUGER
BARBARA
KRUGER
BARBARA

MATT KEEGAN

INVENTORY PRESS

ROGALAND KUNSTSENTER

CONTENTS

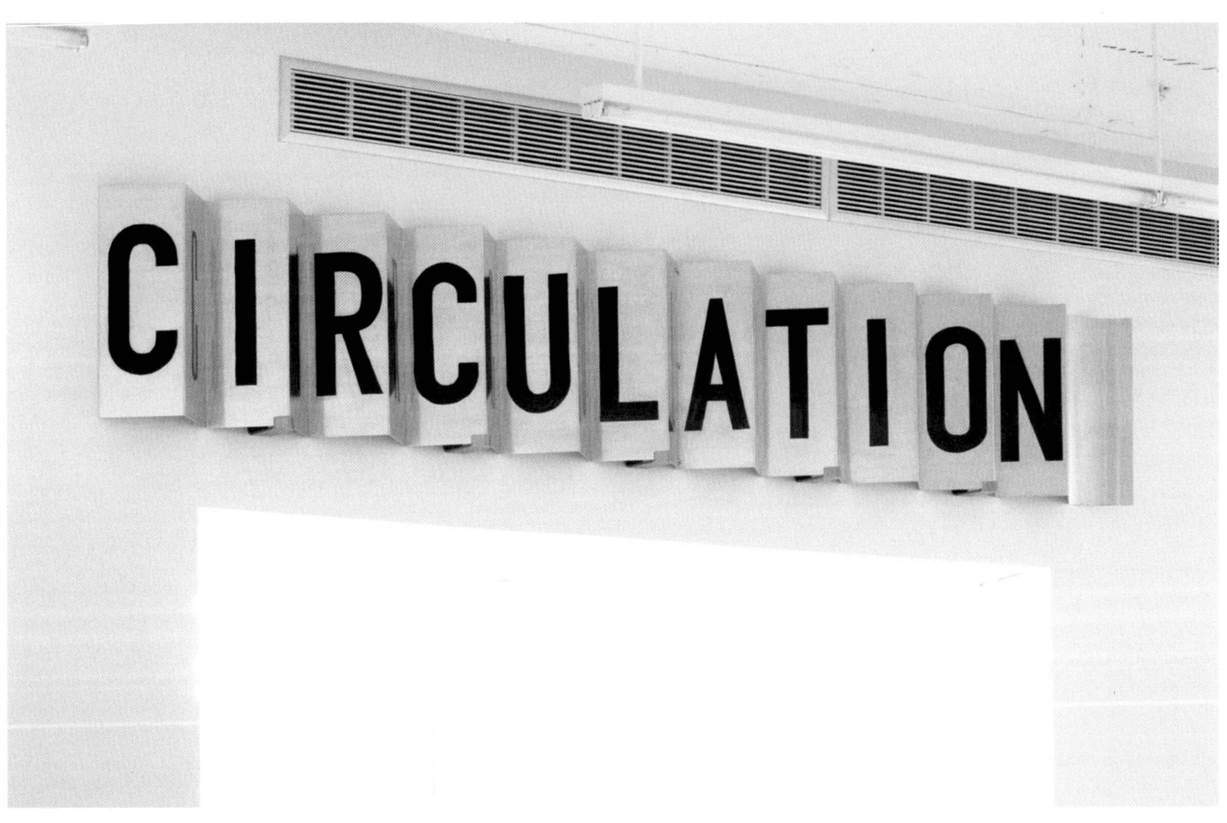

Circulation, 2011. Enamel paint on aluminum. 19 x 8 x 120 in (48.3 x 20.3 x 304.8 cm).

INTRODUCTION

Geir Haraldseth

Art, like language, does not have much meaning until it is utilized, either in conversation or context. Matt Keegan's work deals with both language and conversation among people, materials, circumstances, sites, and histories. This publication highlights some of these conversations through two essays, by art historian Tom McDonough and artist and writer John Miller; interviews with the artist; and contributions from Keegan's collaborators, peers, and friends Uri Aran, Anna Craycroft, Leslie Hewitt, James Richards, and Sara VanDerBeek. These texts all draw upon the rich material that is Keegan's work, creating a conversation contained within this book's covers. A work of art is usually viewed within the context of the gallery space and has its own way of being experienced and read. Keegan conceived of this publication as a site in itself, where the work can be read within the specific spatial dispersal of the book format, drawing heavily on the potential his work has to access ideas about dialogue and his interest in publications and the printed word. The images have been selected in dialogue with the writings, where the hierarchy of information is in flux.

Keegan's keen interest in publications has manifested itself in many different ways, and he's produced many collaborations made in dialogue with other artists, writers, and thinkers. I remember picking up *A History of New York*, an artist book that was part of Keegan's exhibition from 2011 "I Apple NY." The book is a pictorial history of the city where Keegan has spent most of his life and is based upon the rich PBS documentary by Ric Burns, *New York*. Each page in the book contains a single image tapped from the New York Public Library and represents a moment in New York history. The wordless book added another layer to the exhibition as a whole, but was also a work of art in its own right (available for $35). Keegan probably would not insist that the book in front of you is to be considered a work of art, but it is more than an exhibition catalogue—not a catalogue raisonné, but it functions as a vivid contemplation on Keegan's output beyond the gallery space. As a work of art has little meaning outside of a context or a dialogue, so Keegan shows how he is constantly in dialogue with the world around him. This publication marks a specific point in time; the book in your hand offers an appealing adventure and a different approach to the artist monograph, drawing upon a wide net of references to come up with something relatable in scale, but unique in approach.

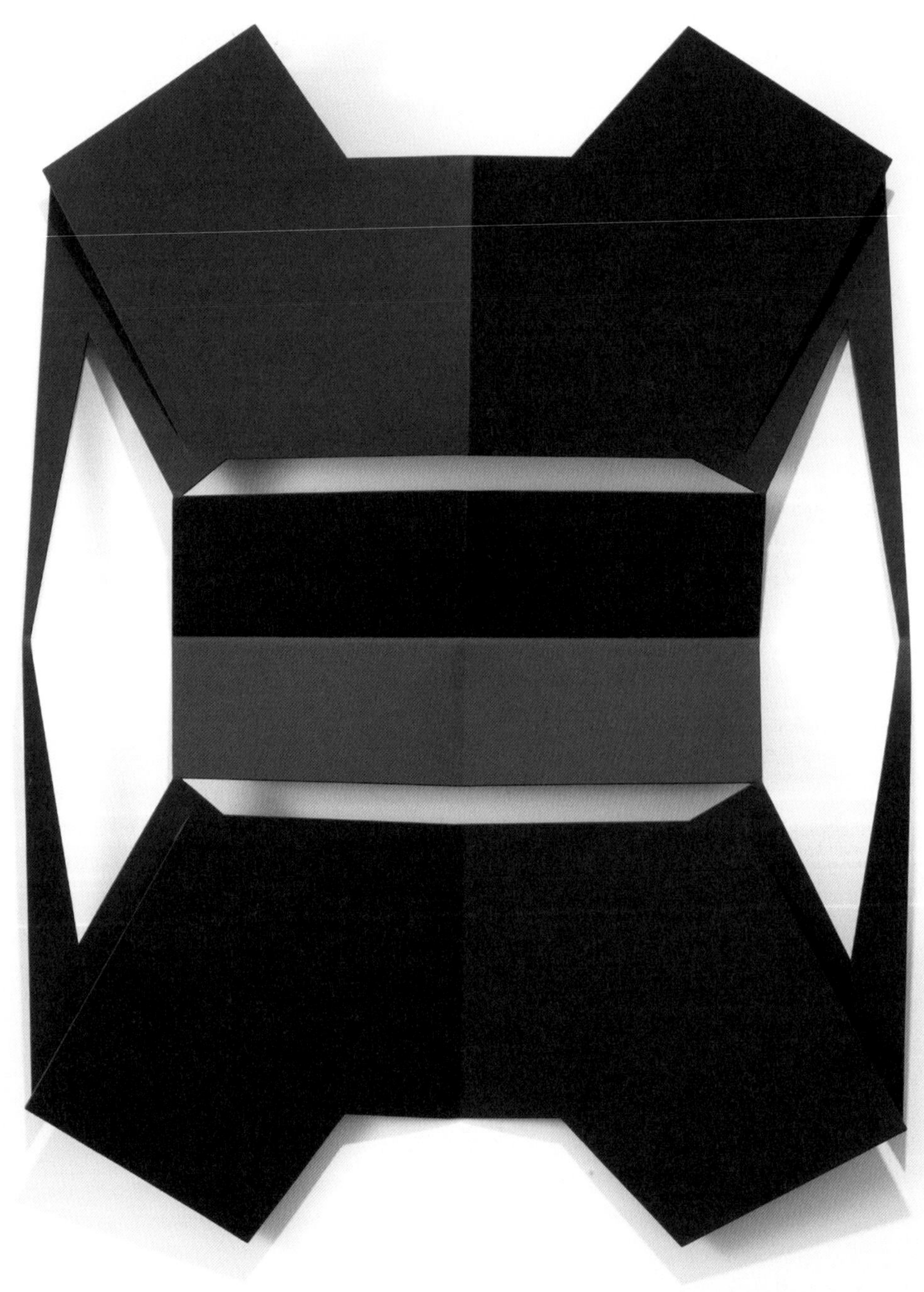

Untitled (Navy), 2014. Powder-coated steel. 32¼ x 23⅜ x 3 in (81.9 x 59.4 x 7.6 cm).

COMMON PLACES READY MADE

Tom McDonough

In fall 2013, Matt Keegan visited a New York gallery exhibition of works from the 1970s by American sculptor Anne Truitt (1921–2004), an artist whose subtly colored vertical wooden totems have been the subject of significant critical revaluation over the last decade or so. It was a striking encounter: "I knew the totems," he would later explain, "but that exhibition opened up a whole other realm of Truitt's work—drawings, paintings, and horizontal, floor-based sculptures that especially struck me. I bought *Daybook*, Truitt's first collection of journal writings, that afternoon." A year later, when he exhibited new work of his own two blocks from the site of Truitt's show, he made one of her steles, *Landfall* (1970), the centerpiece of his installation, her pale-blue tower standing in the middle of the room surrounded by Keegan's photographs and wall reliefs (see 10–13). Formally, it functioned like a fulcrum, a pivot around which the rest of the room, and the viewer, revolved. Conceptually, however, its function was more enigmatic, for despite the obvious respect Keegan has for this artist, his work would seem to refute Truitt almost point by point.

Their differences are perhaps clearest in the two steel wall reliefs Keegan exhibited, *Untitled (Navy)* and *Untitled (Neon)* (both 2014)—cut, folded, and splayed forms that bear the traces of their digital origin in "randomly generated paper cutouts" that are then "enlarged, laser-cut in steel and machine-bent to approximate" their prototypes.[1] Most obviously, the very quality that seemed to draw Keegan to her work—its subtle color—served to distinguish them. Instead of her carefully calibrated range of tones, his reliefs were single-hued, direct in midnight blue and neon yellow. And if, in Truitt, one always senses the paint that covers her wooden forms as a distinct layer on top of the sculpture's substructure, in Keegan's reliefs, color and structure seem to be one, thanks to his use of powder coating, which produces a characteristically hard finish. In this manner, embracing a certain industrial facture, Keegan adheres to what he calls a "vernacular minimalism" much more than did Truitt, who always retained her tie to the hand in her sculptures. But the three-way relationship between Keegan, Truitt, and Minimalism is more complicated than this, and is ultimately articulated around a more central issue than that of color.

Regardless of Truitt's problematic relation to Minimalism, one quality she undoubtedly did share with her contemporaries in this group was the unmistakably anthropomorphic quality of her work. A column like *Landfall*, standing at just over six feet high, encourages the viewer to compare its vertical bearing and its dimensions with those of his or her own body. Michael Fried called attention to this aspect of Minimalist sculpture when, in a crucial passage of *Art and Objecthood*, he described such work as "something like a surrogate person—that is, a kind of statue." He indicated three grounds for such reasoning: the first having to do with the size of Minimalist objects, which are generally scaled to the human body; the second with the ways that "literalist ideals of the nonrelational, the unitary, and the holistic" find their closest analogues in everyday life in "*other persons*"; and the last with how its "apparent hollowness . . . the quality of having an *inside*—is almost blatantly anthropomorphic. It is, as numerous commentators have remarked approvingly, as though the work in question has an inner, even secret, life."[2] The two *Untitled* steel wall reliefs Keegan exhibited along with Truitt's column precisely lack this reference to the human body, this "quality of having an *inside*."

As suggested above, the paper cutouts at the origin of these works were arbitrarily generated. "I fold the paper into quarters and cut the paper without a specific image in mind," Keegan explains. "However, I only select the resultant shapes that look like things, or parts of things, that exist in the world."[3] What those things might be depends to some degree on the viewer. One critic has likened them to "abstracted pieces of clothing, hard-edged Rorschach tests, or perhaps cutting-edge shields," while the artist himself tends to see references to the body, with the reliefs "appearing like armor or another form of garment."[4] But garments and armor are not bodies but claddings for the body, and ones that have their source in the flat form of the pattern—in contrast to the presence of the Minimalist stele, these reliefs seem haunted by an absence suggested in their ambiguous, clothing-like forms that hover between two and three dimensions. Two precedents—one personal, the other art historical, would seem to govern the logic of these works. The first is Keegan's childhood experience of working alongside his maternal grandmother, a seamstress, "as she translated her patterns to make dresses for my sisters based on photos in various fashion magazines."[5] The second is Marcel Duchamp's *Nine Malic Moulds* (1914–15), a study for the mechanical domain of the *Bachelors*, the lower section of his *Large Glass*. Originally known as the *Cemetery of Uniforms and Liveries*, it figures the bachelors as nine masculine types—gendarme, delivery boy, priest, and so on—specified only by their characteristic uniforms. These "molds" appear as hollow shells or dressmakers' patterns, producing an ambiguity between exterior and interior, an ambiguity that similarly extends to masculinity itself, since these masculine—"malic"—molds also compose the feminine "Eros' Matrix," in Duchamp's description.[6]

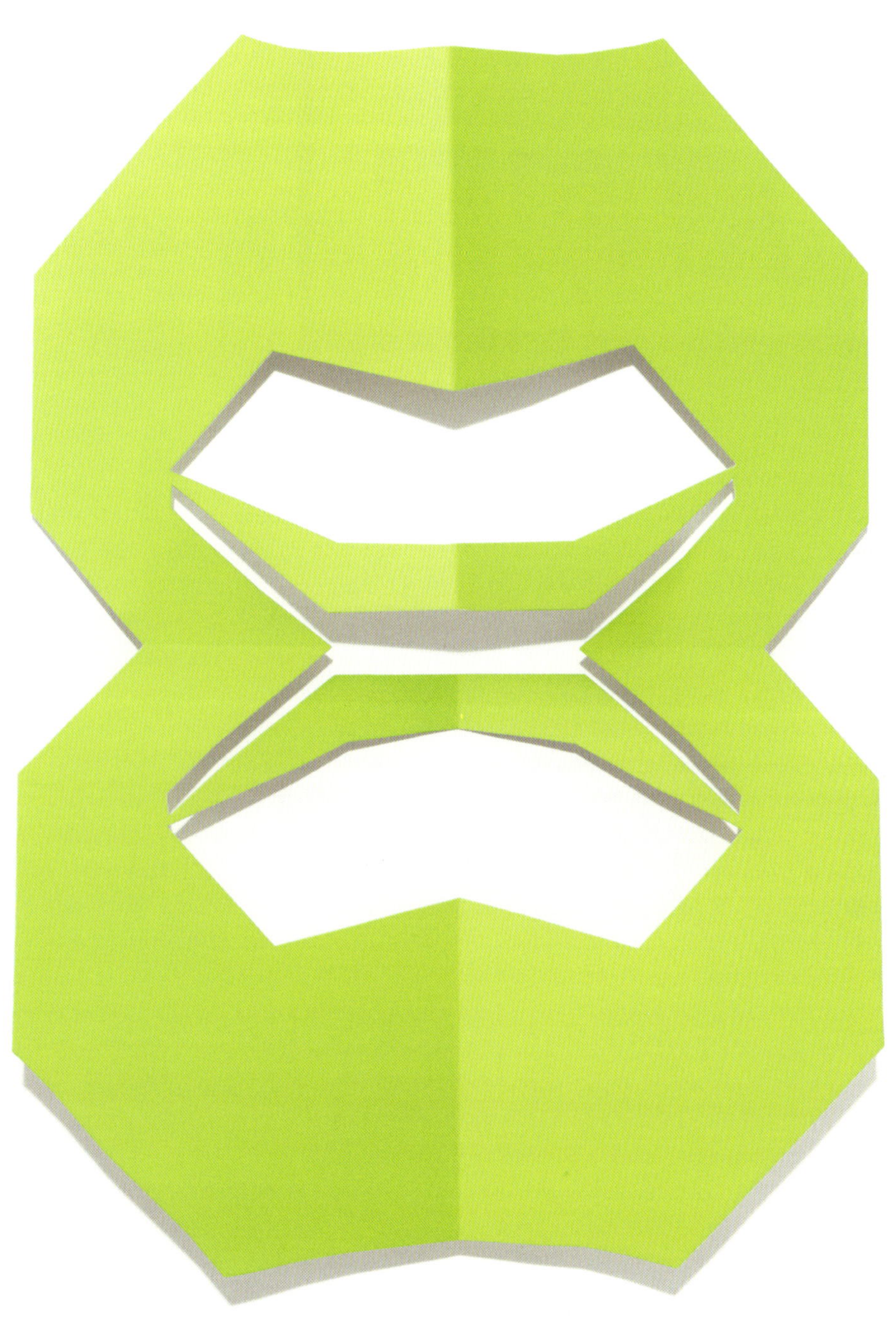

Untitled (Neon), 2014. Powder-coated steel. 32⅞ x 22½ x 4 in (83.5 x 57.2 x 10.2 cm).

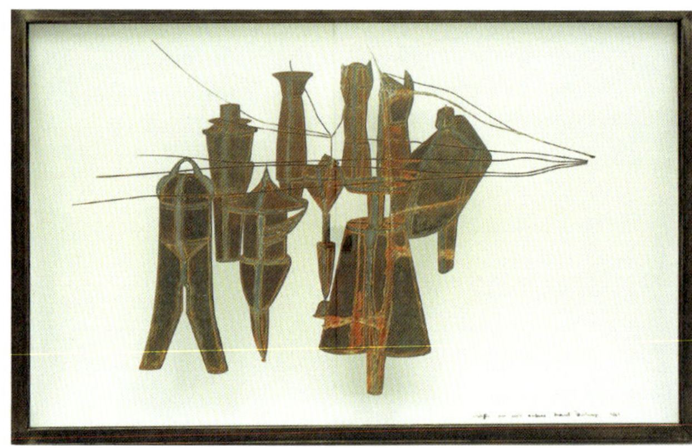

Marcel Duchamp, *Nine Malic Moulds*, 1963. Color photograph between glass. 2½ x 40¼ in (64.8 x 102.2 cm). The Norton Simon Museum, Pasadena, CA.

The play between malic and matrix, masculine and feminine, livery and tailoring seems equally to be at work in Keegan's wall reliefs, although without the clear erotic connotations of Duchamp's piece. Instead, it is translated into the unstable opposition of industrial manufacture and their origins in fragile, cut-paper forms. The term Keegan uses to describe these forms is *template*, which in its semantic instability seems entirely appropriate. On one hand, it simply refers to the mechanical process of their fabrication, their cutting and shaping—although the fact that each is a unique object betrays the potential for larger-scale production implicit in the template. On the other hand, however, "template" makes reference to Keegan's other interests and ties these works to his larger project: namely, to the realms of graphic design and publishing, in which a template indicates a pattern or a layout that can be replicated. Such a template acts as an open field, a ground from which a range of meanings and forms might be generated. Although his distinctive use of language has disappeared from these more recent works, to the extent that they retain a sense of their origins in folded paper, it still haunts their page-like form. Not a body, then, but a surface of inscription—this is the non-anthropomorphic resonance of the reliefs. Perhaps we can say they await language, not unlike the flash cards made by Keegan's mother.

Indeed, the large set of flash cards made by his mother to assist in her English adult education classes constitutes one important source for his thinking about language and form. Cutting out photographs from magazines and store catalogues, she assembled a vast repertoire of cards intended to assist her students in correlating word and image, along the lines of a grade school primer. The stock photography she used was itself a kind of vernacular readymade, but Keegan was fascinated precisely by its ambiguity, by the difficulty in linking image and text: "Each card points to the lack of immediate legibility, and thus the complexity, that her collection attempts to stage."[7] That is rather comically apparent in *"N" as in Nancy* (2011), the looped, two-channel video of his mother naming her own flash cards, an experiment that becomes something akin to a Rorschach test. We see her on the left, the cards on the right, each filmed against a white backdrop, as in an instructional video. As each image appears, she identifies its corresponding word in a deadpan, if sometimes slightly annoyed, tone of voice. Some of the correlations are obvious, but many others are humorously opaque. Yet far from seeing this illegibility as a liability or weakness, Keegan understands it as indicative of the creative capacities of the linguistic system: in his words, it is a matter of the "productive misuse" of a given cultural vocabulary.[8] The multiplicity of potential meanings becomes "a generative activity" that "could eventually formulate a compelling visual lexicon."[9] *How is an Alphabet a Mother? (after GB)* (2011), an alphabet of twelve-inch-high steel letters that lean against the wall at floor height, emblematizes the same point. Language, or grammar, is tied to the maternal in what structuralist linguistics would have called its generative qualities. Letters, images, and words share the logic of the matrix, endlessly producing meaning along a sliding range of signifiers.

Hence the title of the exhibition in which these works were displayed: "Lengua," meaning "language" in Spanish, as in *lengua materna*. Duchamp, too, was of course fascinated by the generative powers of language and the multivalent quality of words, the way puns break the "demand for a single, fixed meaning" and instead express "multiple meanings within a solitary linguistic construction."[10] That this was tied to the question of the maternal-as-matrix for Duchamp as well might be indicated by the choice of his female alter ego, Rrose Sélavy, to author his wordplays. In addition to the video and alphabet, "Lengua" also included several cut-steel sculptural reliefs into whose surfaces have been cut idiomatic phrases, drawn from what might best be characterized as the stock repertoire of early twenty-first-century conversational and bureaucratic speech. *It Goes Without Saying* (2011) is a circle just over two feet in diameter, made of thin steel liquid coated in a bright egg-yolk yellow, with the title's phrase—repeated eight times in decreasing size—cut into one half of the disc. *He Said, She Said* (2011) is floor-bound and flesh-colored, while the traffic-light green, polygonal *Nothing to Declare* (2011) projects from the wall like a signboard. Keegan's rather expressionless commonplaces are a far cry from Duchamp's clever punning, but he nevertheless shares his forebear's preoccupation with the limitless fecundity of language.

In each of these works, our attention is undoubtedly first drawn to the statement itself. Keegan has described such phrases as "specific in how vague they are."[11] In this regard, "it goes without saying" is particularly redolent,

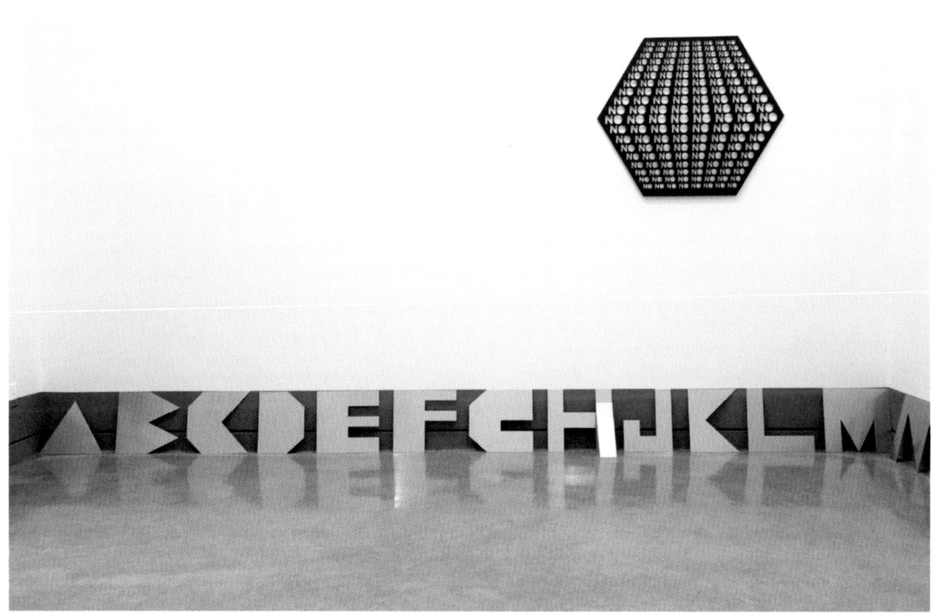

Installation view, 2011. *Lengua*, Altman Siegel, San Francisco, CA.

not least because its idiomatic usage indicates that something is obvious or, more specifically, that a speaker believes that his or her interlocutor will already know what one is going to say because it is so generally understood or accepted. Of course there is a paradox at the heart of this formula, since we inevitably go on to state precisely what we have just insisted need not be said, and it is this curious excess or imprecision that seems to pique Keegan's interest. Many of the phrases cut into his sculptures in this 2011 series share something of this quality. "He said she said"—a more contemporary urban idiom than "it goes without saying"—suggests the un-decidability of certain romantic conflicts, indicative, Keegan has said, "of a kind of impasse where subjectivity is immediately addressed but to no clear end."[12] Such capabilities of language, to designate vagueness or uncertainty with precision, are as central to the artist's practice as they are to our commonplace linguistic realm. Sculptural materialization and repetition play key roles in these "Lengua" works, the words of a simple phrase assuming a strangely hermetic significance as they are transformed into an object. However familiar the language might be, its uncommon appearance outside the space of the sign or the book, along with its being cut from sheets of steel, guarantee a degree of defamiliarization. In this way, Keegan takes the most standardized of our linguistic tokens, the clichés

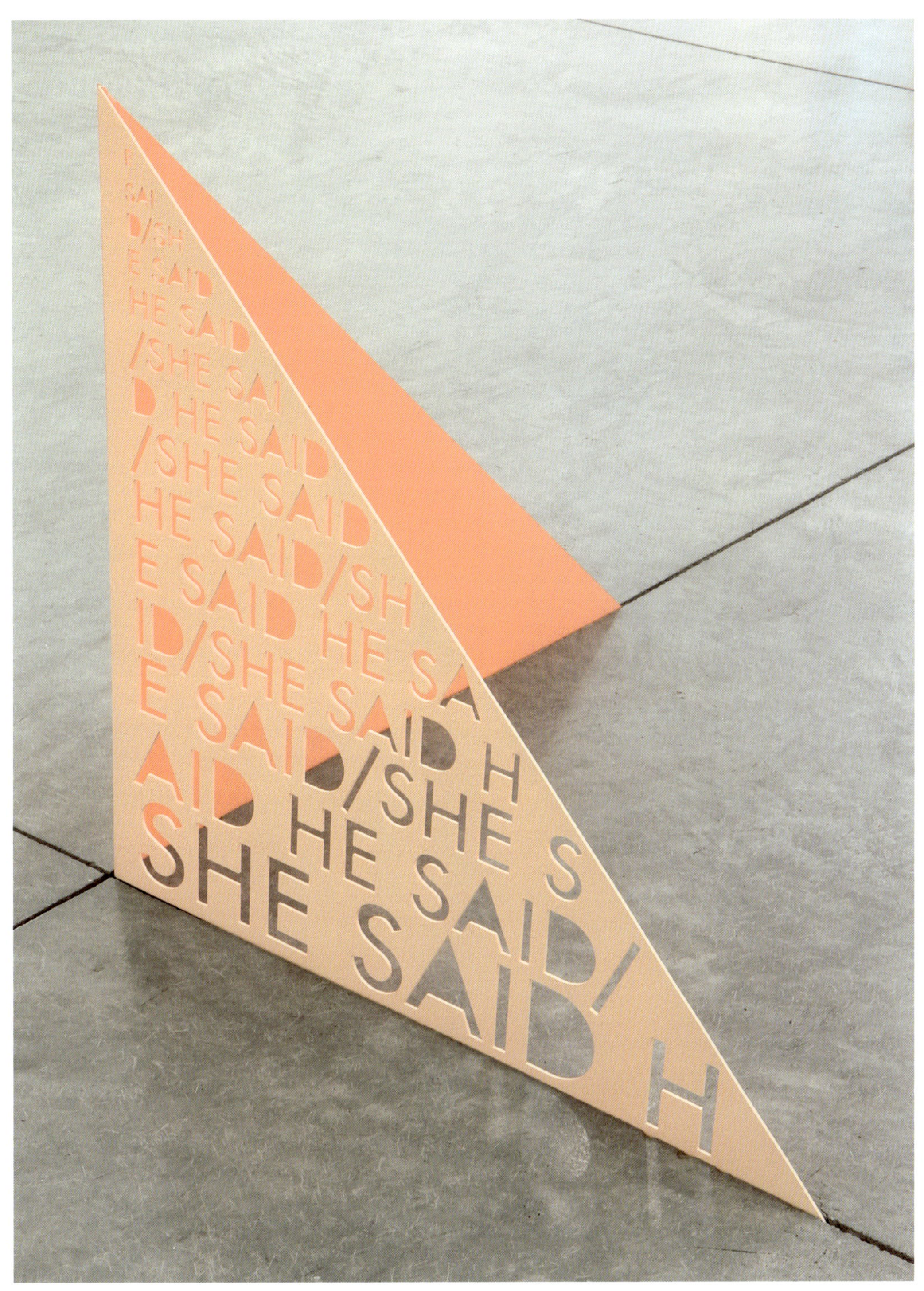

He Said, She Said, 2011. Spray-finished laser-cut steel. 30 x 30 x 30 in (76.2 x 76.2 x 76.2 cm).

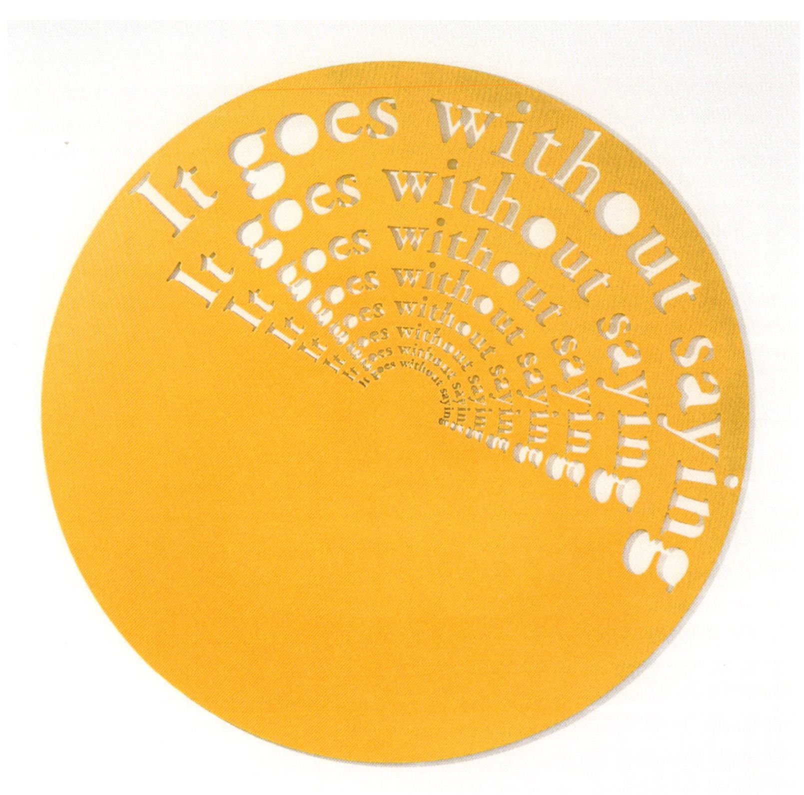

It Goes Without Saying, 2011. Spray-finished laser-cut steel. 27 x 27 in (68.6 x 68.6 cm).

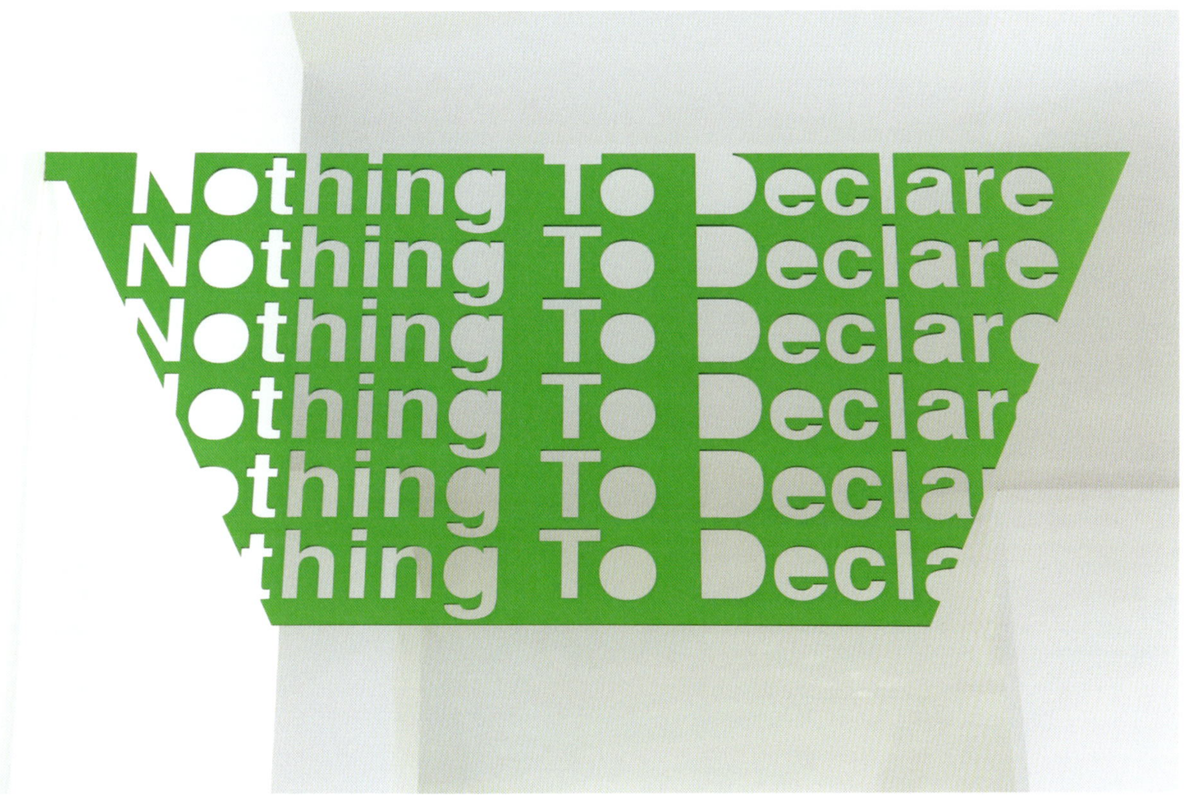

Nothing to Declare, 2011. Spray-finished laser-cut steel. 16 x 34 in (40.6 x 86.4 cm).

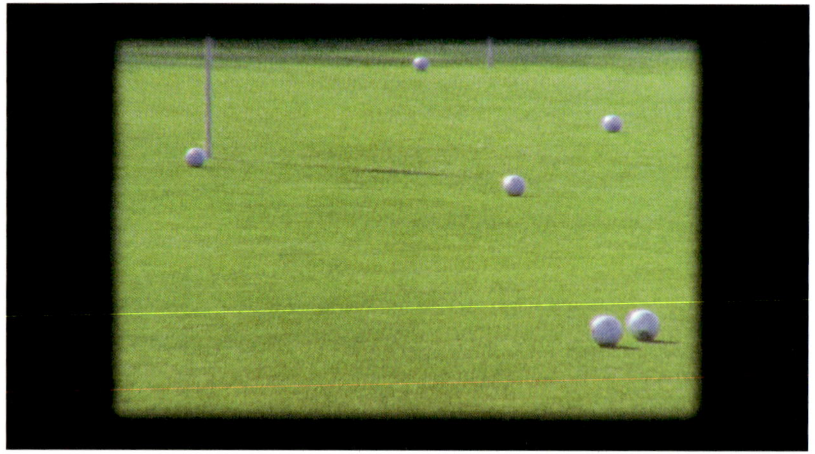

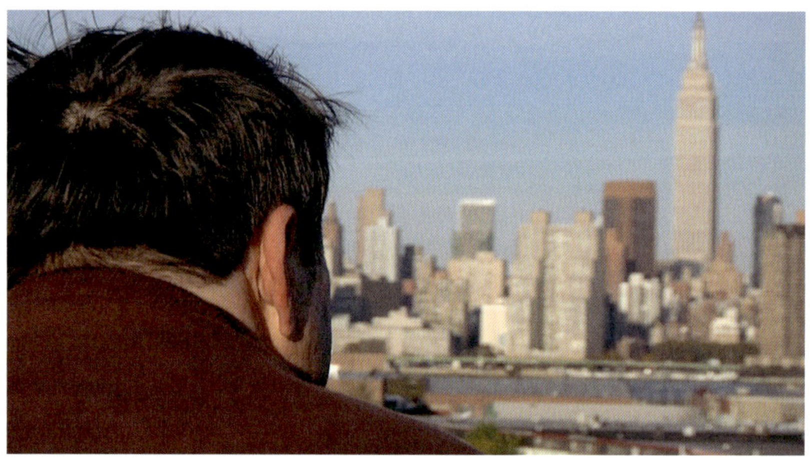

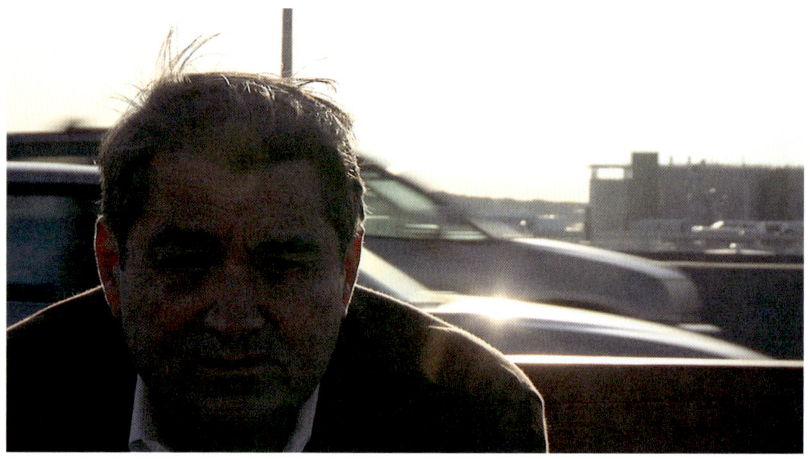

Biography/Biographer, 2011. Documentary video. 9 minutes.

of everyday speech, and turns them against themselves. Indeed, the commonplaces of Keegan's work are most frequently phrases of negation that declaratively perform their strangely abstract rejections—"no no no," "nothing to declare," "it goes without saying." It is difficult to decide whether in them we are witnessing the banality of daily conversation raised to the level of poetry or the aesthetic renunciations of high culture brought down to the level of reified speech—this, too, is part of their categorical "specificity in vagueness."

During that same year, 2011, Keegan paired language as maternal archive with a paternal order: the city, urban planning, and public space. His exhibition "I Apple NY" explored the city as another form of archive, with *"N" as in Nancy* finding its masculine counterpart in *Biography/Biographer* (2011).[13] Keegan made this video with his father, who recounts his time as a teenager working as a caddy at a suburban golf course frequented by Robert Moses, the "power broker" who reshaped greater New York in the years prior to and following the Second World War, according to his autocratic vision. In contrast to the straightforward, direct address of Keegan's mother to the camera, this video purposefully takes up some of the tone and gestures of historical documentary, particularly as the brothers Ken and Ric Burns have codified them in their popular television productions. Keegan has spoken of the importance of the latter's public television documentary *New York: A Documentary Film* (1999–2003) for his conception of this show, a debt most clearly felt in *A History of New York*, a pictorial compendium of the city's history covering the same four-hundred-year span as Burns's series, assembled almost exclusively from images found in the New York Public Library's now-defunct picture collection.

What kind of archive is this? If it consists largely of representations of public events, of the city's historical turning points, it nevertheless shares the quality of the vernacular readymade or the stock image with the flash cards of "Lengua," in that history is here reduced to a set of visual clichés. In speaking of "I Apple NY"—the title derives from a collaboration with graphic designer David Reinfurt, riffing on Milton Glaser's iconic promotional logo of the mid-1970s—Keegan has remarked on his wish to produce "something that's accessible to the viewer," and of course texts like that of the Burns documentary are premised on a form of accessibility, clarity, and understandability that make them suited to a wide viewing audience.[14] They construct a totalizing viewpoint that unifies history into a grand, overarching narrative with an implicit—or not so implicit—message of inspiration and hope. Keegan's book and the video *Biography/Biographer* mimic this form without ever simply repeating its mythologizing of history.

In titling the exhibition "I Apple NY," Keegan appropriates and fuses two of the city's most recognizable logos: Glaser's "I Love New York" design of

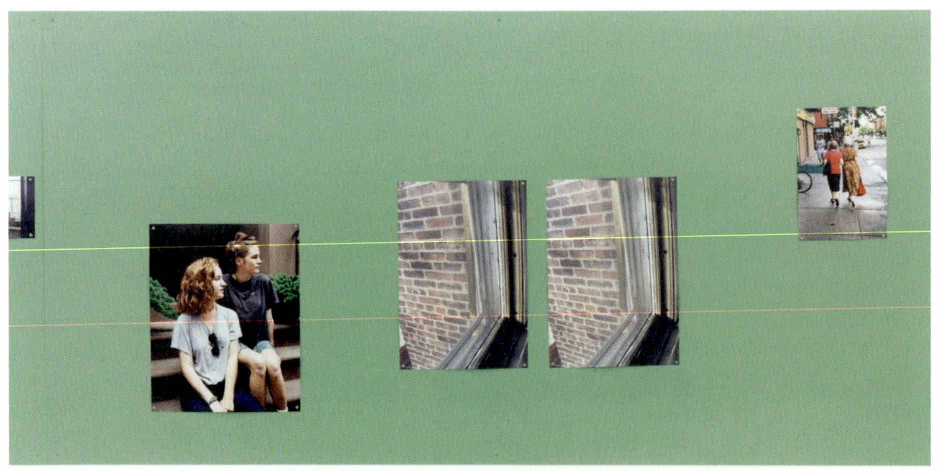

Untitled (Group 11), 2011. Four c-prints attached with magnets to steel panels spray-finished in Aluminum Green. 48 x 96 in (121.9 x 243.8 cm).

1977 and the moniker of "the Big Apple," which, while originating in the early twentieth century, owes its popularity to a campaign by the city's Convention and Visitors Bureau from the early 1970s. Working with Reinfurt, Keegan substitutes Glaser's "heart" with an "apple"—actually, with fellow designer Will Holder's apple design for the Amsterdam-based contemporary art institute de Appel—and the result once again is a curious illegibility-in-legibility. We recognize the phrase almost instantly, but meaning is short-circuited, and while we can certainly read the new logo, we cannot make much sense of it. "I . . . like how it confuses the legibility," Keegan has remarked. "What does it mean to apple something?"[15] The logo, that near-ubiquitous figure of our late capitalist landscape in which language and commodity most closely intersect, is rendered mute, or at the least diverted from its semantic univocality.

If documentary is governed by totality and closure, by the confident grasp of a story and its sure retelling, then fragment and metonymy govern the logic of Keegan's work. A large *Untitled frieze* (2011) circled the gallery walls in "I Apple NY": four-by-eight-foot panels of sheet metal in a continuous horizontal strip, painted the official color palette of New York City's transportation infrastructure (e.g., George Washington Bridge Gray), onto which photographs

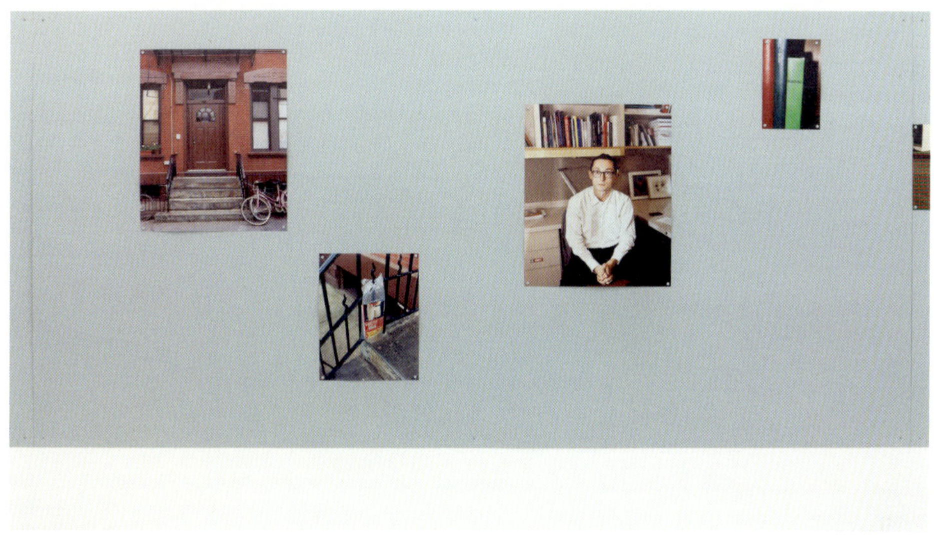

Untitled (Group 4), 2011. Four c-prints attached with magnets to steel panels spray-finished in George Washington Bridge Gray. 48 x 96 in (121.9 x 243.8 cm).

have been attached with magnets. The photos, taken by Keegan over the previous year on walks through various nondescript neighborhoods of the city, offer a decidedly unspectacular vision; their grouping seems determined less by any narrative suture than by formal rhythm, as in Group 11, with its doublings: first, of two young women seated on a stoop, then of two images of a window frame and the brick wall beyond and, finally, of two older women, seen from behind, walking down a street. We are offered elements of a language, no doubt, but they resist incorporation into a coherent photographic sentence. This is an archive of sorts, and it possesses the archive's flexibility—there is a strong suggestion that the sixty photographs arranged across the panels could be reordered in any number of different configurations to produce different possible meanings—but it is an archive that draws the public life of the city back into the realm of the private reference, into inscrutability. These common places—sidewalk, mailbox, barred window—resist being pulled into a larger meaning, a story of the city; they instead adhere to what Keegan has called his "meandering logic."[16]

Manhattan's bridges are not so much evoked as engineering marvels—as, say, Ric Burns might do—than as anonymous, nondescript color schemes,

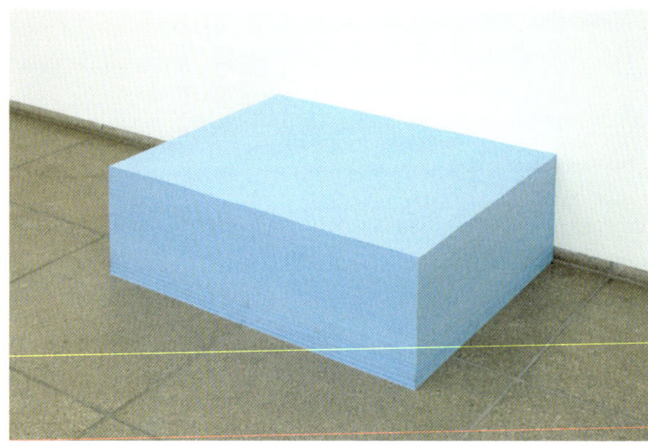

Felix Gonzalez-Torres, *Untitled (Loverboy)*, 1990. Blue paper, endless supply. 7 ½ in at ideal height x 29 x 23 in (19.1 x 73.7 x 58.4 cm). Hamburger Bahnhof, Museum für Gegenwart, Berlin, Germany.

a readymade palette. But these sheet metal panels are also literal bridges, blank sheets that serve as unifying ground for the poetic, photographic text. They are, we might say, paternal/maternal templates, malic in their industrial material and palette, and matrixial in their generative capacity to produce new meanings and combinations. This sort of template appeared early on in his work, with his use of four-by-eight-foot boards of Sheetrock as the basis of text works such as *Real Life* and *Meryl Streep* (both 2008); rotated ninety degrees to the horizontal, those boards became the metal panels of 2011's *Untitled*. Hand-cut, the Sheetrock becomes *Lattice (Open)* (2014), a repeated four-by-eight-foot architectural unit serving as a ground for the display of works in his show with Anne Truitt, as does *Pink Lattice* (2014), installed for an exhibition in San Francisco. In each case, it serves as a space of inscription, like a page on which individual texts—words, photographs, wall reliefs—may be written.

More recently, the city's street architecture, glimpsed in some panels of *Untitled*, appears as a species of found sculpture, captured by the photograph: in *Curb* (2014) our attention is drawn to the rather battered meeting of sidewalk and street; in *Yellow Grate* (2014), the steel grill found under our feet is rotated to the vertical and placed on the wall; *Paved Grate* (2014) does something similar. In each instance, Keegan aligns the sculptural with the horizontal, with what lies at our feet, and with the nameless architecture of the urban milieu. The regular pattern of *Yellow Grate*—so familiar to the denizens of Manhattan's avenues—reminds us that the grid, seriality, and repetition were commonplaces of industrial production before they were the hallmarks of Minimalist abstraction.

Specifically, we could say that Keegan occupies something like a fourth moment of the American reception of Minimalist sculpture. If the first moment, in the 1960s and '70s, largely understood it in terms of the constitution of a phenomenological subject binding spectator, sculpture, and architectural surround, subsequent moments have reread its forms through a decidedly more cultural lens. In the mid-1980s, during a second moment of reception, artists and historians—from Dan Graham and Peter Halley to Anna Chave—called attention to its alignment with corporate décor and the display of control and power. Developing from this, the third moment in Minimalism's post-history saw feminist and queer practices of the early 1990s—from those of Andrea Zittel to those of Felix Gonzalez-Torres—critiquing and reconceiving the gendered terms of its sculptural forms. Keegan's work, in its embrace of readymades and commonplaces, ushers us into what is definitively a fourth moment of the movement's reception, alongside contemporaries such as Shannon Ebner and Virginia Overton. With it, Minimalism is approached as something like a template from which to generate new forms, its enclosed black boxes opened to become planes, its masculinist vocabulary transformed into something generative, matrixial.

NOTES

1. See press release for "Matt Keegan and Anne Truitt," September 12–October 25, 2014, Andrea Rosen Gallery, New York, NY.
2. Michael Fried, "Art and Objecthood," in *Minimal Art: A Critical Anthology*, ed. Gregory Battcock (New York: E. P. Dutton, 1968), 128–129.
3. Keegan, in correspondence with the author, February 3, 2015.
4. Andrew Russeth, "Matt Keegan and Anne Truitt at Andrea Rosen," *ARTnews* (December 2014): 112; and Keegan, in correspondence with the author, February 3, 2015.
5. Keegan, in correspondence with the author, February 3, 2015.

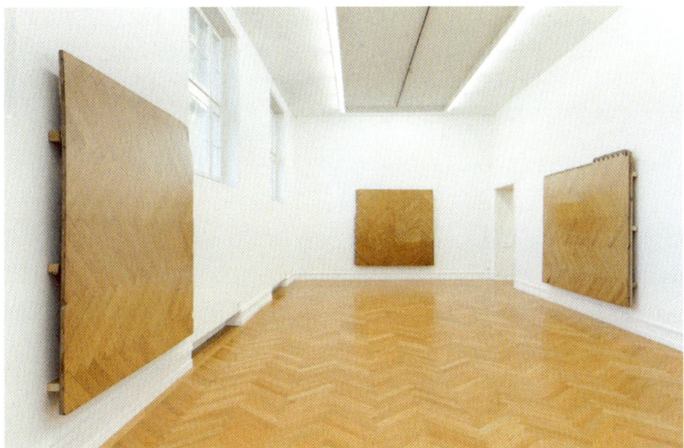

Virginia Overton, Installation view, 2013. "Virginia Overton," Kunsthalle Bern, Bern, Switzerland.

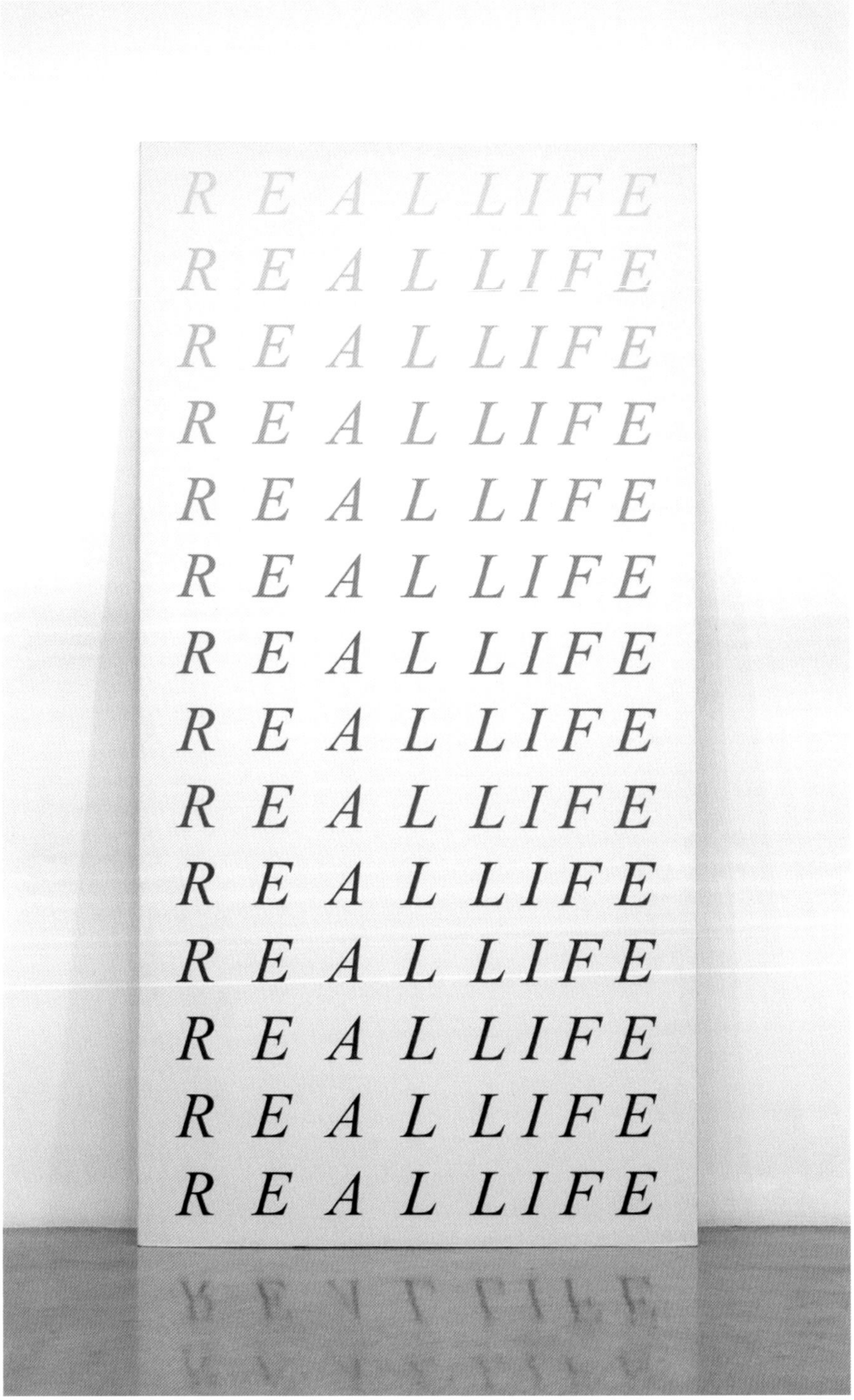

Real Life, 2008. Latex and acrylic paint on cut and peeled Sheetrock. 96 x 48 in (243.8 x 121.9 cm).

6. On this play of ambiguities, see Dalia Judovitz, *Unpacking Duchamp: Art in Transit* (Berkeley and Los Angeles: University of California Press, 1995), 69–70.
7. Keegan, "Lost in Translation: Do you see what I read?," *MAP–Journeys in Contemporary Art*, no. 24 (Winter 2010): 47.
8. Keegan, quoted in Zak Kitnick, "Federal Blue & Deep Cool Red: A Conversation with Matt Keegan," *Idiom Magazine* (2012), accessible at http://idiommag.com/2012/11/federal-blue-deep-cool-red/.
9. Keegan, "Lost in Translation," 47.
10. Gavin Parkinson, *The Duchamp Book* (London: Tate Publishing, 2008), 51. Beyond Duchamp, we might also note the relationship of these works to earlier forays into language by artists such as Bruce Nauman, although shorn of the overt aggression found so often in the latter's word-based works.
11. Keegan, quoted in press release for "Lengua," November 3–December 17, 2011, Altman Siegel, San Francisco, CA.
12. Keegan, quoted in press release for "Lengua."
13. *More Like* (2012), a text work made for an exhibition at The Kitchen, New York, in late 2012, thematizes this play between maternal and paternal registers, repeating "More like Mother / More like Father" in a manner formally similar to the repetitions of the "Lengua" works.
14. Keegan, artist's talk, Carpenter Center for the Visual Arts, Harvard University, November 13, 2014.
15. Susan Barber, "It Takes Two: Matt Keegan," *Acne* (2011), accessible at http://acne.openingceremony.us/entry.asp?pid=3423.
16. Keegan, artist's talk.

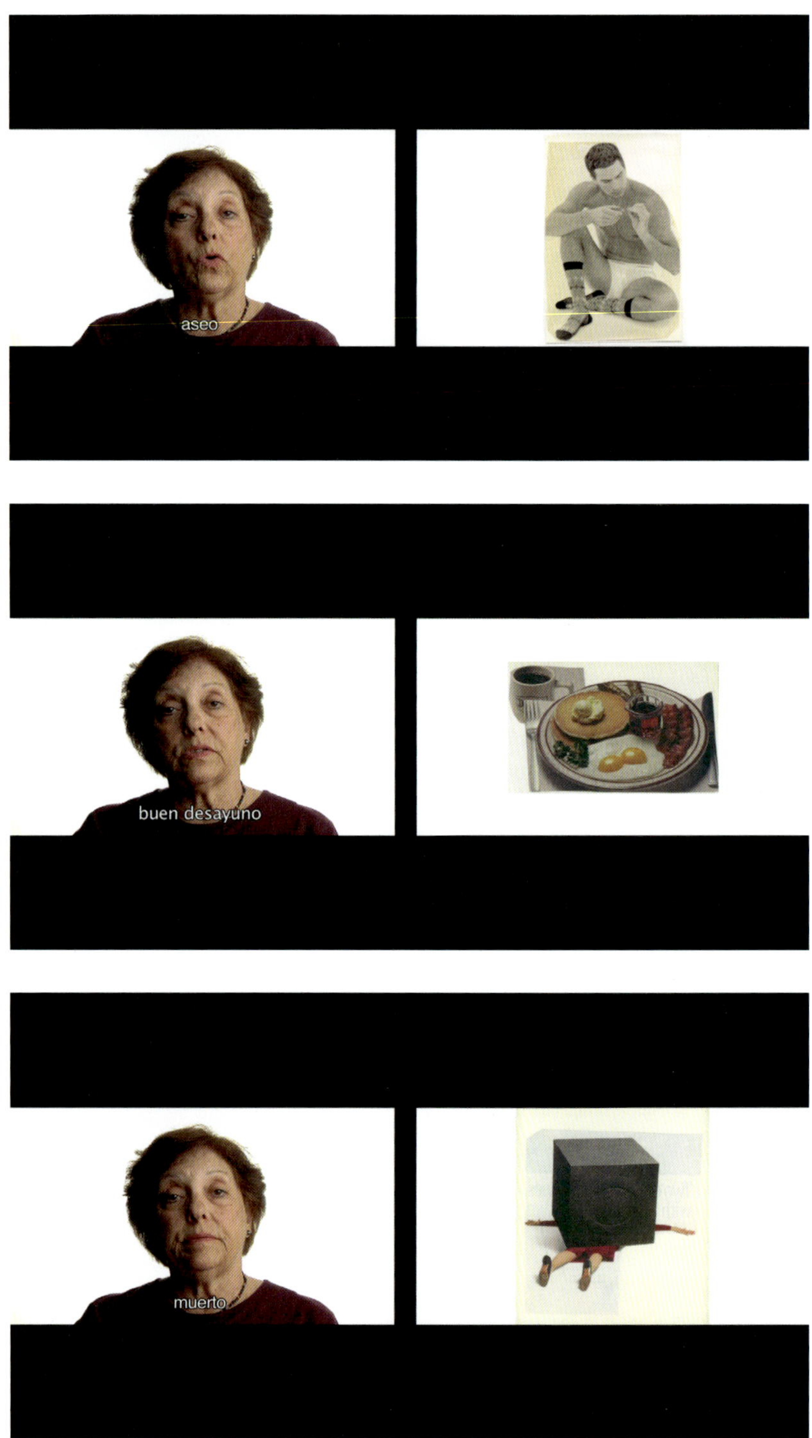

"*N*" *as in Nancy*, 2011. Two-channel video, 3 minutes.

“A IS FOR APPLE.”

John Miller

Where does an artwork begin and where does it leave off? Jacques Lacan cites the potter—the most primordial of all artists—who molds a vase around emptiness. To do this, nonetheless, requires appropriating a certain amount of physical material, clay, from the world. And this appropriation marks a delineation from nature, a second nature composed of language or technology. The correspondences and discrepancies between language, technology, and “the world” from which they sprung took explicit form in Surrealism, with René Magritte’s most famous work, *The Treachery of Images* (1928–29), a painting that features the legend “*Ceci n’est pas une pipe*,” or, in English, “This is not a pipe.” Fourteen years earlier, Marcel Duchamp produced, reproduced—or produced by contextualization—the readymade *Bottle Rack*. As an appropriated work, it raises the question of who does what in an artwork and how to identify and quantify that labor. It may even imply an Adorno-esque idea: that technology is an extension of natural history.

Matt Keegan does not consider his video, *“N” as in Nancy*, to be a collaboration. (And what is collaboration beyond a provisional agreement, an apportioning of artistic labor under the sign, perhaps, of authorship?) Nonetheless, it raises questions about who produces what artistically and, more broadly, about categorization in general. Keegan made the video with his mother, Nancy Keegan, who for many years taught English as a second language, mostly to recent Central American immigrants to the United States. Her appearance in this video, of course, results from an agreement she made with her son to act or to perform in this work. Part of her teaching involved using homemade flash cards whose images she clipped from various magazines. Matt Keegan’s video considers how she chose these clippings.

The video appears in a split-screen format. On the left, Nancy Keegan pronounces a word or a phrase in English. A Spanish-language subtitle appears at the bottom of the screen. On the right, various flash-card images appear, often cut in irregular shapes, perhaps to crop out the advertising or editorial copy that once surrounded them. Here, “learning English” is implicated in the ability to read an image. Since pictures are so rarely denotative, the unstated component of this learning process is learning to see an image the same way the teacher does. This implicit demand for consensus is ideological.

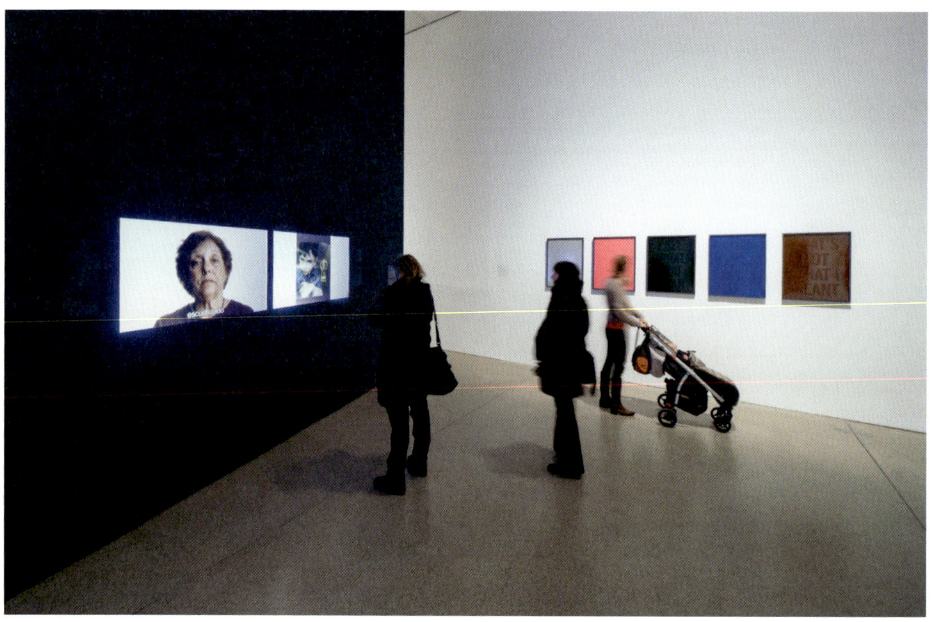

Installation view, 2011. "Found in Translation," Deutsche Guggenheim, Berlin, Germany.

Linguistically, much of how and why one would read an image in one way, as opposed to another, revolves around the segmentation of the semantic continuum. Notably, the linguist Benjamin Lee Whorf linked these divisions to the principle of relativism in language. If the linguistic categorization reflected in words is relative, this implies not only that one language is not transparent to another but also that linguistic competence is bound to specific cultural and historical milieux as well. It points to the materiality of language as a social process.

Parallel to Whorf's theory and in the wake of structuralist inquiry, the idea of pure visuality gave way to the notion that all images are always already invested with language. This is hardly a simple question of word versus image. In his essay "Lost in Translation: do you see what I read?," Keegan considers Will Holder's graphic design for the Dutch art institution de Appel. Holder based his design on the phrase "A is for Apple." Keegan observes: "I am not a semiotician, and I do not believe in universalist concepts, yet this basic correlation appears to have near-global legibility. A is for apple. Apple is A. The two are interchangeable."[1] Through consensus, this seems to be true, but the close correlation obscures the complexities of recognition. According to common sense, letters stand for sounds, and words are built from these. It's not so simple.

Letters represent families of related signifying sounds, i.e., phonemes. Moreover, the sonic character of phonemes is not absolute, but contextual. And, of course, language is more than vocabulary. One could dissect further, but the point is that what seems to be transparency in language is primarily a matter of habituation and collective recognition. Further: if a sign is the relation between a signifier and a signified (or referent), what exactly is a signified? A discrete thing? A class of discrete things? And if it's a *class*, which implies a level of abstraction, what are the criteria for inclusion and exclusion?

We might say that, rather than collaborating, Keegan appropriated his mother's flash cards. These flash cards, however, are not something she *created*. And no one starts from nothing. Sure, she selected the images, clipped them, glued them to poster board, and even applied a laminate film on top to insure that they would stand up to repeated handling. But because these images are all photographs, they constitute a particular kind of information with—to paraphrase Vilém Flusser—only an arbitrary relationship to their material substrate. Flusser called the photo a "contemptible flyer," something someone could easily wad up into a ball and discard. Interjecting photos between language and the world, moreover, complicates the signifier/signified relationship because now there would appear to be at least two signifiers: the word and the photograph. Can one signifier be the signified of another signifier? This is a question that Joseph Kosuth's *One and Three Chairs* (1965) addresses. Kosuth's work presents a physical chair together with the word *chair* and a photograph of the same, leaving one to wonder about the connection between these elements. Moreover, according to Flusser, photographic meaning is inherently unstable. Rather, residing in the photograph as a "thing-in-itself," photographic meaning is formed by distribution channels:

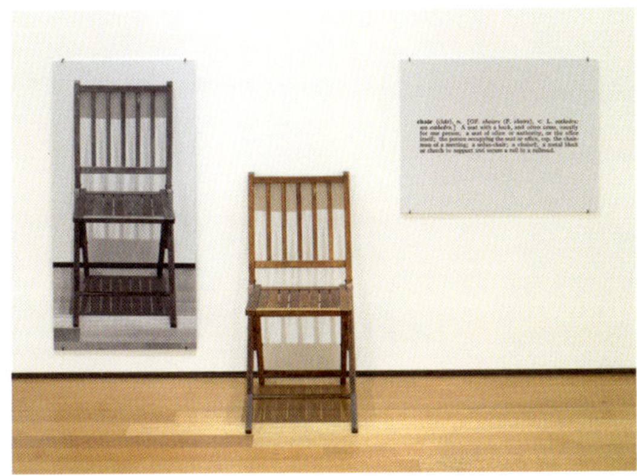

Joseph Kosuth, *One and Three Chairs*, 1965. Wood folding chair, mounted photograph of a chair, and mounted photographic enlargement of the dictionary definition of "chair." 32⅜ x 14⅞ x 20⅞ in (82.2 x 37.8 x 53.0 cm). MoMA, New York, NY.

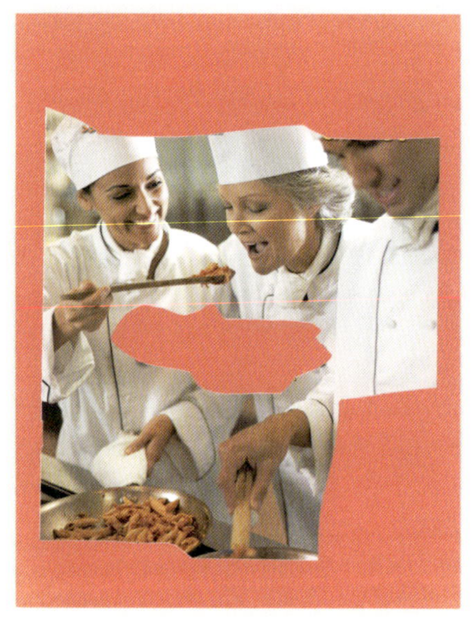

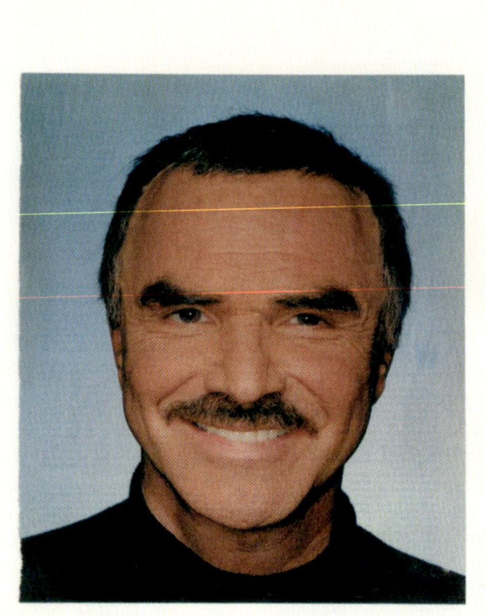

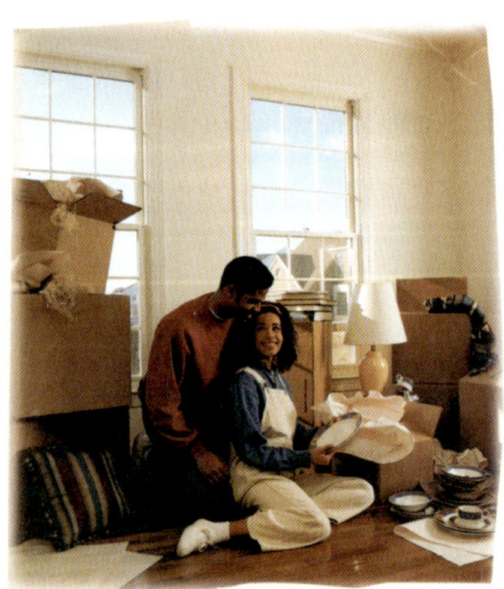

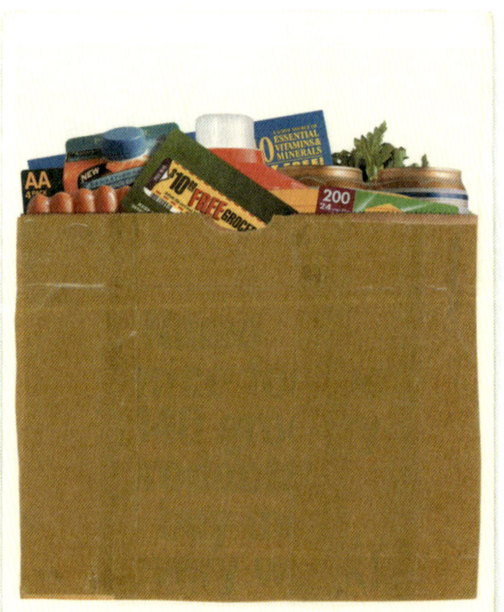

Flash cards made by Nancy Keegan to teach English as a second language to high school and adult ed students.

The photograph of the moon landing, for example, can slip from an astronomy journal to a US consulate, from there onto an advertising poster for cigarettes and from there finally into an art exhibition. The essential thing is that the photograph, with each switch-over to another channel, takes on a new significance: The scientific significance crosses over into the political, the political into the commercial, the commercial into the artistic. In this respect, the division of photographs into channels is in no way simply a mechanical process but rather an encoding one: The distribution apparatuses impregnate the photograph with the decisive significance for its reception.[2]

A similar sequence of switchovers occurs in *"N" as in Nancy*: from popular magazine to classroom to art gallery. While the artistic channel promises that the signifying process will be self-reflexive, it's impossible to set a beginning or end to this signifying chain. In this, is it not willful and perverse to restrict the production of meaning to the so-called decisive moment of pressing a shutter release? Rather, philosopher and educator John Dewey's conception of the artwork (as opposed to art object) as a collective endeavor promises a more comprehensive grasp of how contemporary culture produces meaning.

Keegan notes that his mother used a portrait of a smiling Burt Reynolds to illustrate the word *happy* and suggests that it could portray *actor*, *masculine*, or *mustache* just as well. None of these, however, register Reynolds's status as a sex symbol, someone who posed naked—one of the first men to do so—for *Cosmopolitan* in 1972. Factoids like these haunt Keegan's selection from his mother's selection of images. None of them ever achieve the bland universality of the paradigmatic apple. Rather, they are pictures that aspire to some ill-defined normative function while inevitably falling short, in part because of their datedness, namely their inability to anticipate what "normal" would look like in the near or distant future. Keegan exploits these outré qualities to undercut the premise of normativity. That is why, like Walter Benjamin and like the Surrealists, he turns to the "just past," a temporal margin that is no longer in fashion, yet not yet historicized. It's hard to describe what this looking backward does better than Keegan:

Although it was not her intention, my mother's archive generated a peculiar and particular snapshot of the cultural moment of the 1990s. With the recent US midterm elections [2010], Democratic and Republican candidates belabored the rhetoric of "championing the working class." Ageing somewhere between 10 and 20 years old, these middle-class attuned images cast a light on the dramatic decline of this representative constituency that maintained stability during the Clinton

> years (cue images of saxophones, cigars, free trade, and memories of financial potency). The cropped and hand-cut photos capture a cultural moment that is frozen within their laminate. In keeping with their perplexing utility as a language-learning tool, the images also present an equally provocative and perverse record of a decade's mediated dreams and desires. Whether requesting a student or museum viewer to engage this set to elicit memory or meaning, this collection proposes endless speculation. Such basic looking becomes quite complex, and what you see requires endless permutation to determine what you may get.[3]

Working in tandem with nostalgia (for viewers who may be old enough to remember) is the sense of disenchantment that Benjamin ascribed to the "just past." One reason he valued this particular temporality is because, in this phase, the commodity relinquishes its utopian promise. And, with that, one begins to see the phantasmagoria of capitalism in a different light.

In 1977, Lacan famously pronounced, "The word is the death of the thing." In this, he implies that "the thing" is the real, that which cannot be sublimated, the past that cannot be recovered, and what is ultimately equated with the infant's union with the maternal body. When Marcel Proust attempted to convey just such a recovery (ironically) through literature, it was less articulable experiences, i.e., taste and smell, that triggered epiphanies in his narrative. For Proust, involuntary memory was a moment when the past was not remembered but relived, in its originary plentitude. And it is a more modest, yet comparable, coalescence that the flash card—by virtue of recall, flashing up or flashing back—holds as well. Of course, the flash card is bound to a deliberate attempt to memorize words, but the images it relies upon always call up something more.

NOTES

1. Matt Keegan, "Lost in Translation: Do you see what I read?," *MAP – Journeys in Contemporary Art*, no. 24 (Winter 2010): 47.
2. Vilém Flusser, *Towards a Philosophy of Photography* (London: Reaktion Books, 2000), 54.
3. Keegan, "Lost in Translation," 49.

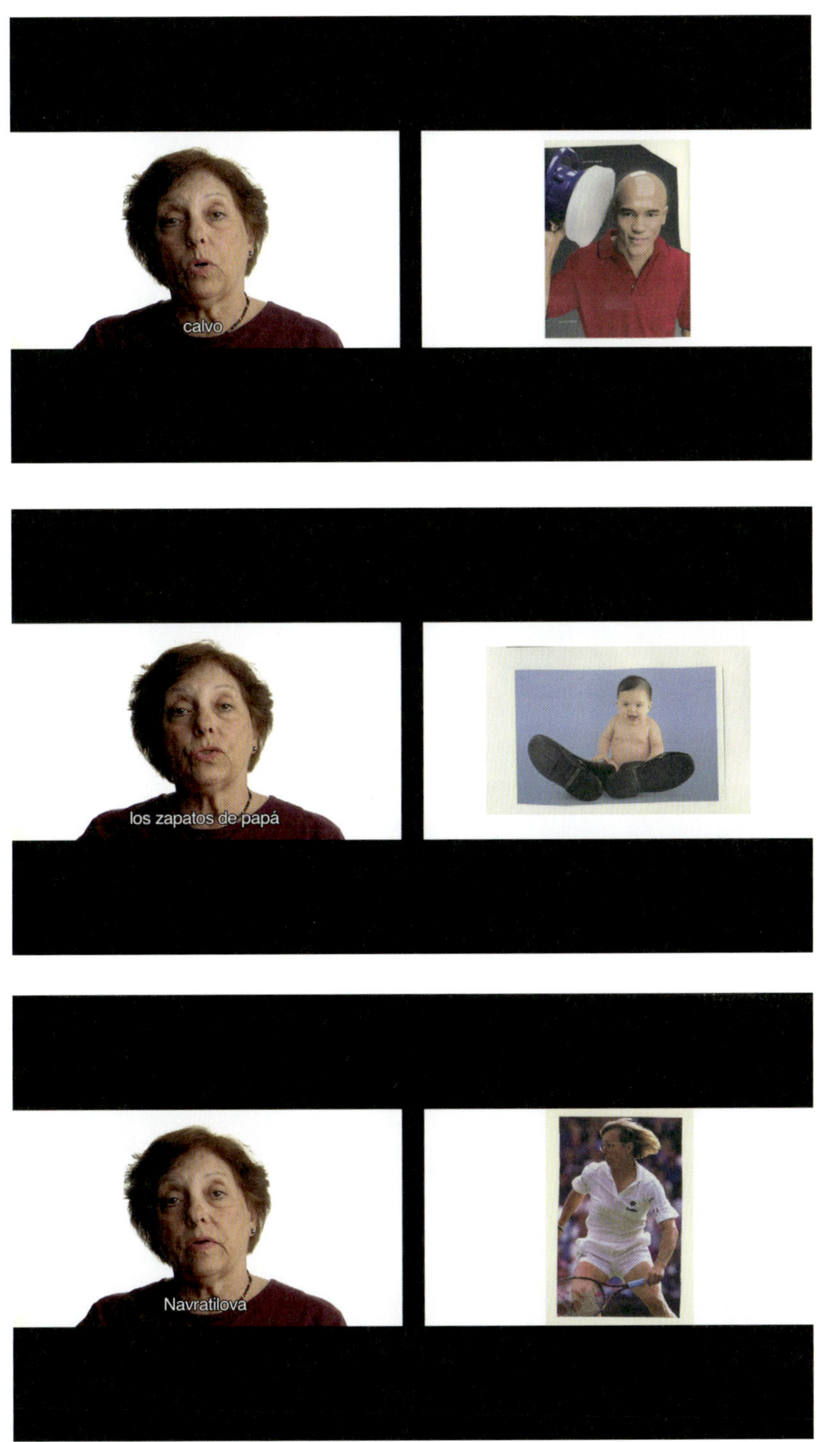

"N" as in Nancy, 2011. Two-channel video, 3 minutes.

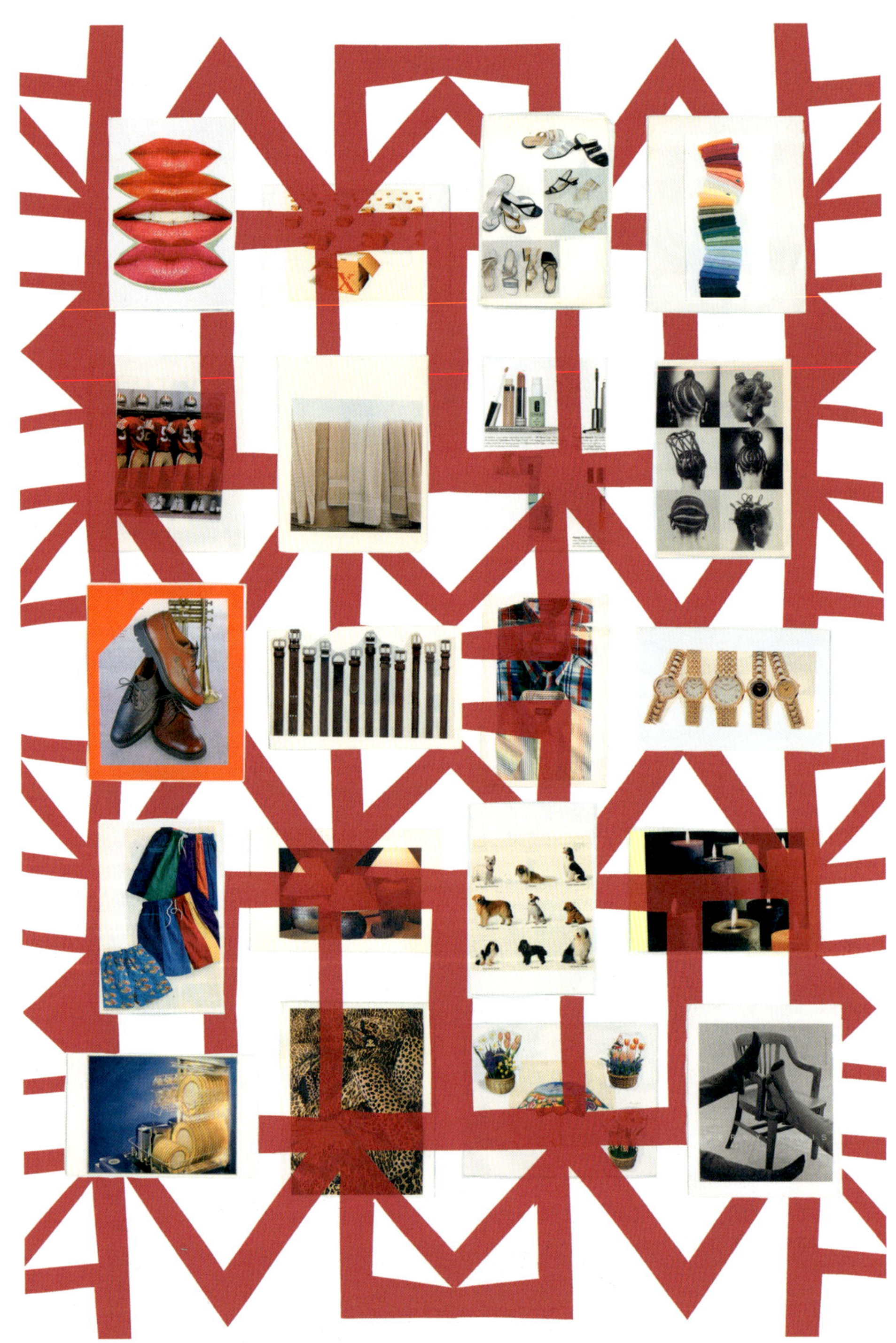

Grids, 2012. Digital c-prints and latex paint on wall. 66 x 44 in (167.6 x 111.8 cm).

WE ARE LIMITED TO AN *I LOVE YOU*

Uri Aran

As part of our coaching into being careful and becoming "golden troops" (also known as crossing guards) in elementary school, somewhere between fourth and sixth grade, we were sent to a simulated driving park where students like us were taught the basic rules of the road.

Basic rule: Follow the rules.

Basic rule 2: You obey traffic rules. You break a rule, you become a pedestrian. That is the punishment—a downgrade from driver to shamed pedestrian.

We all started as drivers, mounted on a small vehicle—a car-looking creature equipped with pedals—to generate movement, somewhat. There was a steering wheel; that was a good thing. It was a car. I was driving a car.

But the best part: it was all in a walled-off park—a life miniatured, a model for an urban driving situation—a freshly painted detour park with roads for cars, crosswalks, warning lights, stoplights, and stop signs.

I was stopped after two minutes. I was made an invisible pedestrian, a creature that has nothing but himself.

I thought (if I remember correctly) that I was great. I'm staying in the car. I clearly remember the excitement, and I'll admit that I would still enjoy it: yellow lines, changing lights, freshly painted signs and a game. I had more belief in a model.

Some kids argued, and by doing so, there lingered the inevitable identical result—you walk from here.

Matt's work is so close to the world from which it borrows that there is an uncanny feeling to it.

Closed and open.

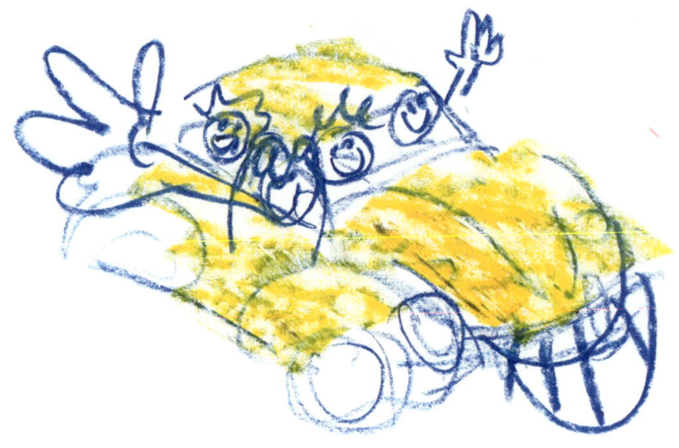

Uri Aran, *Untitled*, 2008. Oil pastel on paper. 14 x 11 in (35.6 x 27.9 cm).

Red and green.

He is the teacher and the pupil. He breaks down systems into different colors, letters, and basic forms. He builds a visual language of how to behave. Without losing loyalty to syntax, he braves the language of authority. By doing so he cancels it, or at least questions it from within. He might put a model next to another model, and by doing so, exposes the implication of what a model can do.

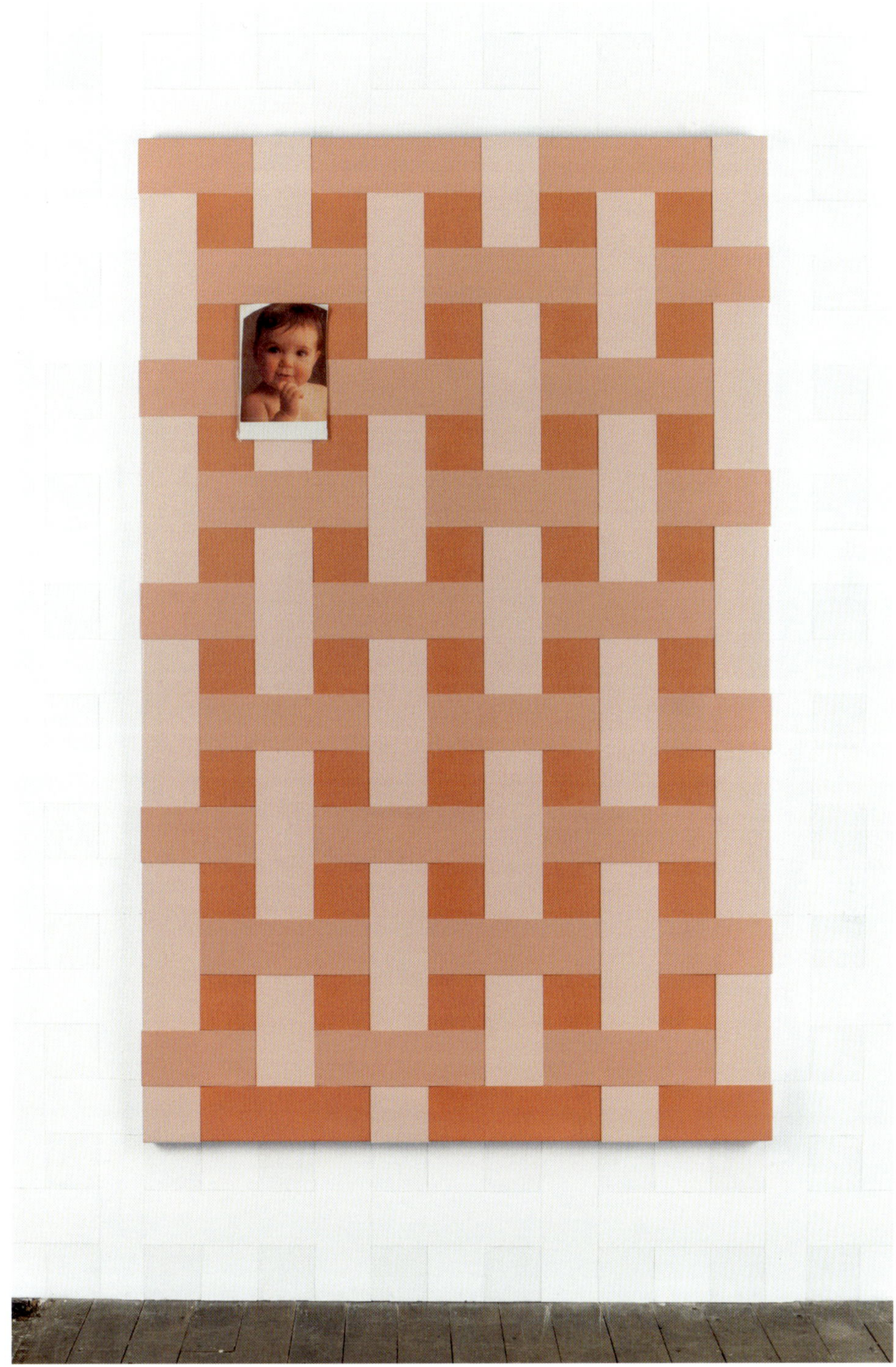

Baby, 2014. Spray-finished steel and laminated flash card affixed with magnets. 72 x 44⅛ x 1 in (182.9 x 112.1 x 2.5 cm).

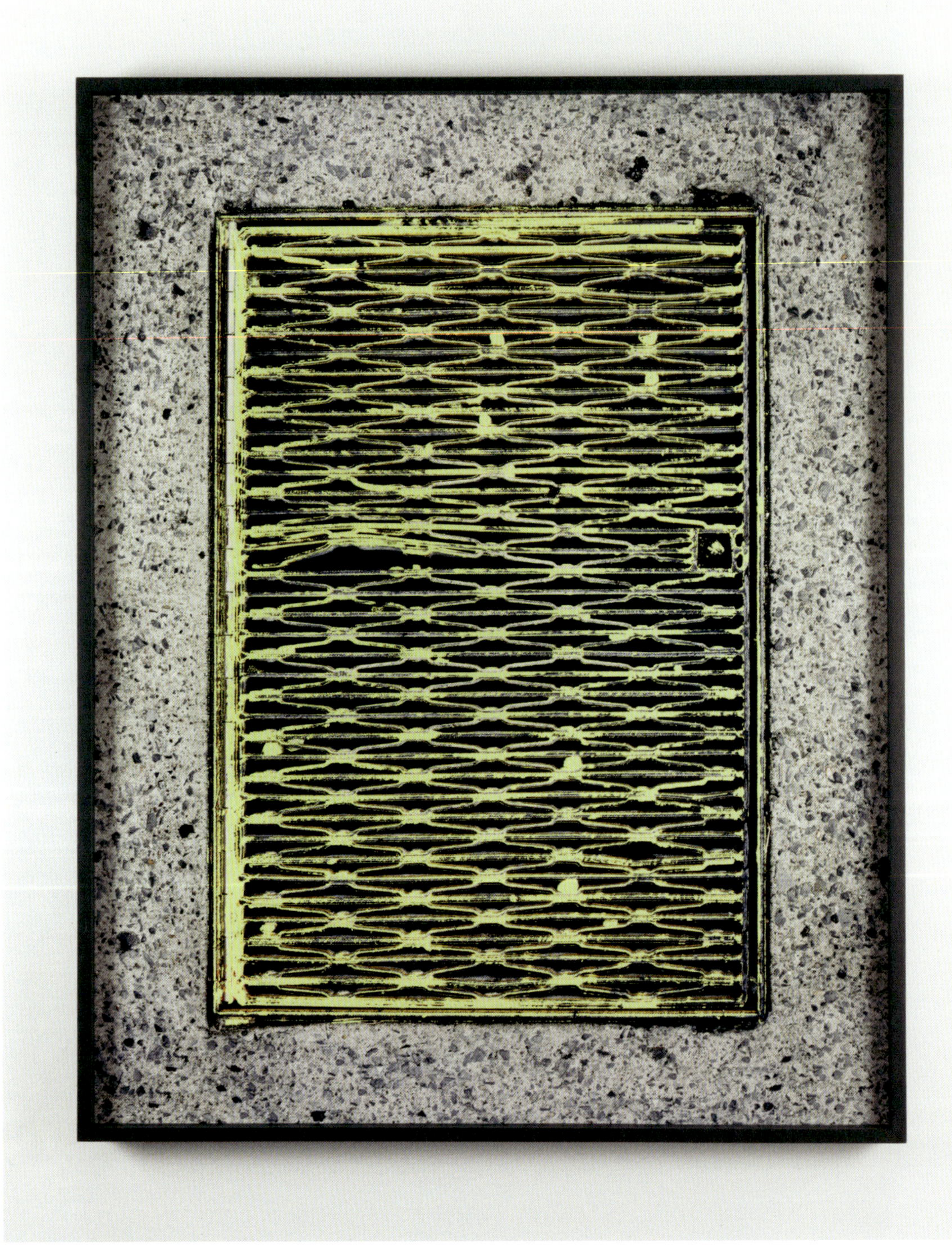

Yellow Grate, 2014. C-print with silkscreen on UV Plexi. 47 x 36 in (119.4 x 91.4 cm).

MIRRORRORRIM

A Conversation with Sara VanDerBeek

Matt Keegan: Before recording, we were talking about mirrors. I'm interested in the shallow depth and deep space of the mirror in relation to works that I've been making by silk-screening a portion of a photograph on top of the UV Plexi of its frame. Thinking about the space between the Plexi and the photograph: it's something that we take for granted, but it is actually material. So, what happens if it's treated as such and becomes a constituent part of the image?

Sara VanDerBeek: The mirror as a shifting space and your consideration of the glazing of a frame opens up thinking about how framed images can become, in some ways, realms of infinite perception. Through your use of Plexiglas as a surface upon which an image is printed, the perception of image and form is constantly shifting. Simultaneously, you are looking through it and in combination with the photographic image. The printed silhouette then acts as a symbol, a surface, and a plane of conveyance to this other shifting realm.

I equate mirrors with photography. I still use an SLR film camera, and the mirror in it is integral to the process of capture. I'd like to hear you speak about your work with the four-by-five camera, in particular, and your work with photography in general. Something that I think is really interesting is the way that you often find sites or objects of interest and initially capture them with your phone, then return later with this larger apparatus to carefully reframe and capture an earlier experience found by happenstance. This, in turn, results in a final image that is choreographed and resolved, yet retains the immediacy of the original moment of observation.

MK: When I'm going from point A to point B between home and studio, home and photo printer or fabricator, I'll see certain things and photograph them with my phone, recording the time and location in the notes section, because the light and the time of day is usually central to why I'm photographing that thing at that time. Then I go back with Lance Brewer, my former student, who has a four-by-five camera, and we shoot that location at the same time of day. I haven't been persuaded to move to digital yet, because there's something in the contact print and the physical stages of editing that I really enjoy, and although the film gets scanned and outputted as a digital c-print, I'm still interested in

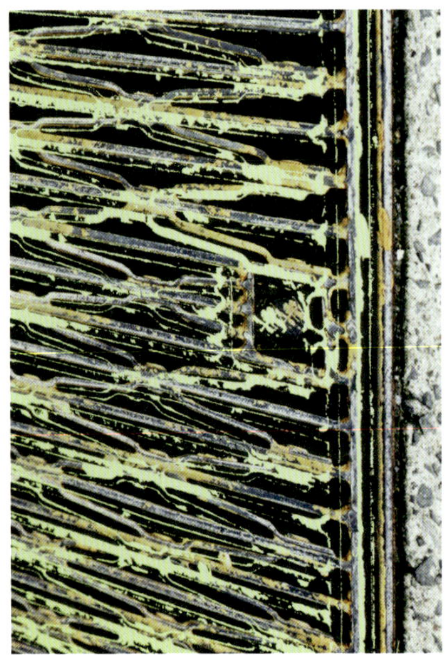

Yellow Grate detail, 2014. C-print with silkscreen on UV Plexi. 47 x 36 in (119.4 x 91.4 cm).

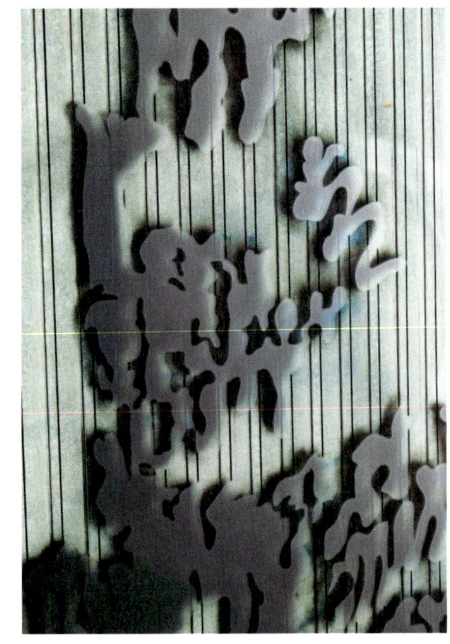

Graffiti Buff detail, 2014. C-print with silkscreen on UV Plexi. 61 x 41 in (154.9 x 104.1 cm).

having a part of that process not be relegated to a screen. Maybe because my interest in photography stems from sculpture and making photos that have a direct relationship to sculpture.

SV: It's interesting to hear you talk about the physical objectness that goes along with the film process, because that is an incredibly important aspect of the process for me as well. But you were talking about how you come to photography from sculpture, and I come to sculpture from photography. I think most people would consider sculpture and photography to be diametrically opposed, but I think they have this ongoing and evolving relationship to each other, which is fascinating.

MK: I totally can see how photographic sight lines and planes lead to your sculptures. They have a similar speed and a quiet presence to them, as I find in your photographs, and tend to have symmetry and scale that function as an interlocutor between your photos and the exhibition space. Imprinting comes to mind with your plaster and wood sculptures, which have patterns incised into their surfaces. There's a clear relationship to a printer's plate, as if a block or linoleum print could be pulled from them. Those sculptures create a ground that one could imagine

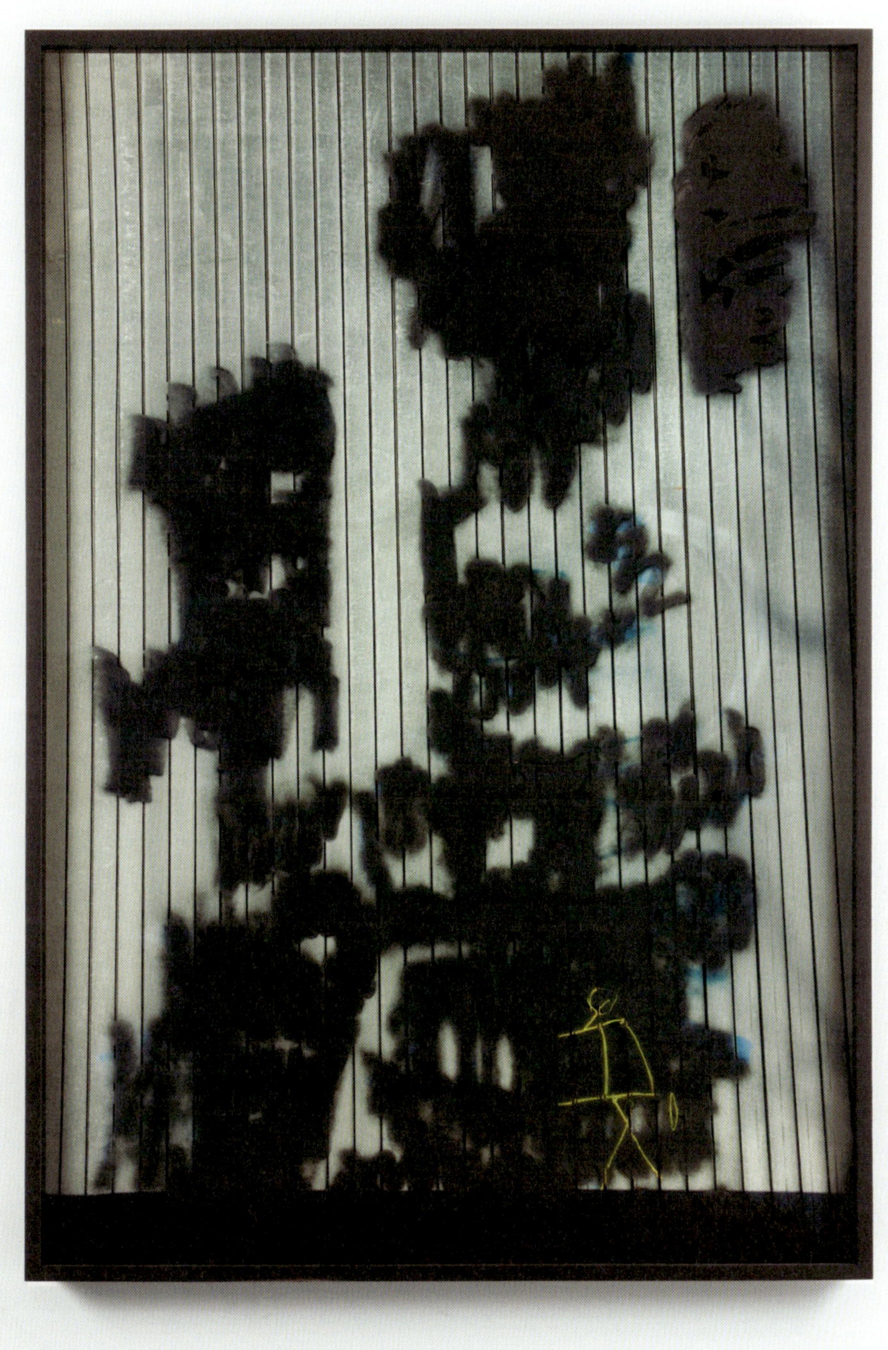

Graffiti Buff, 2014. C-print with silkscreen on UV Plexi. 61 x 41 in (154.9 x 104.1 cm).

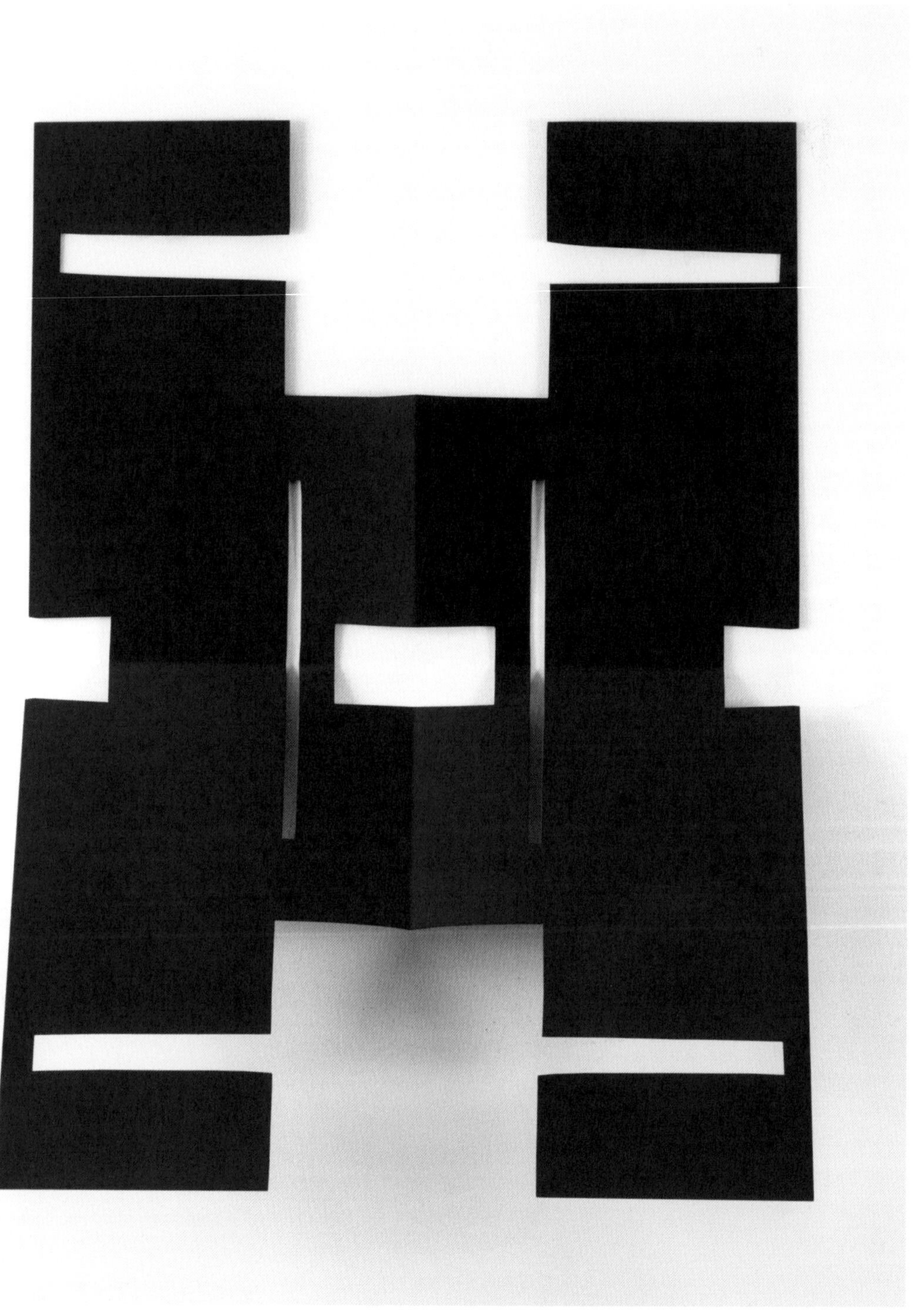

Untitled (Blue), 2014. Powder-coated steel. 32¼ x 23 in (81.9 x 58.4 cm).

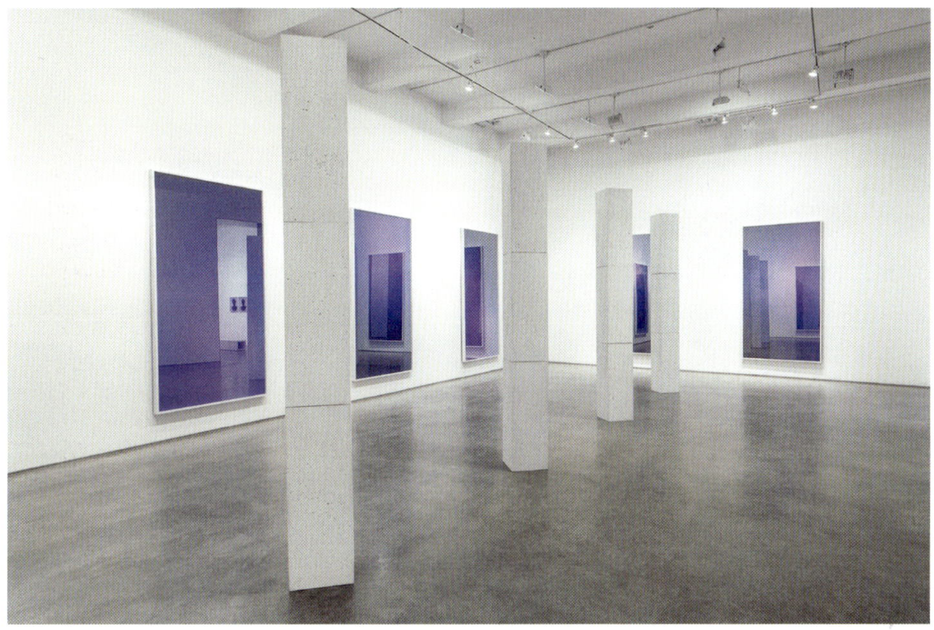

Sara VanDerBeek, Installation view, 2013. "Sara VanDerBeek," Metro Pictures, New York, NY.

not only replicating, but one into which you could etch or emboss. The textural surfaces also have an affinity with my recent Sheetrock work.

SV: I think a lot about that with the casting process; it involves a positive and a negative, and that is very similar to film. I shoot a negative, and it makes a positive print. When I make a mold, I'm often building the negative space to create the positive form. I also like that it's transformational. Throughout the process it shifts from different states of being, and inherent within the cast form is the process of its creation. I think the metal works you have created from cut paper have a similar quality. The process of their making is apparent in a way that expands the presence of the final static object to something that is resonant of an ongoing process of interpretation and movement between states of being. The cut paper is also often slightly off in its symmetry. This is interesting because it is then a pattern with inherent deviations in it. Similarly, you work with pattern often in the overall installation. I'm glad we're getting into this, because I'm interested to hear more from you about how you came to using pattern. What I like about working with patterns is the sense of continuity and continuum within their repeating forms—they are one of the few rare elements that are shared among many of the world's cultures.

MK: Yes—and vernacular.

SV: A vernacular that is quite remarkable; it has been spoken for thousands and thousands of years. Please talk about how you choose the patterns you work with. Are they purely mathematical? Are they inspired by an original source? And the other thing you said that I don't want to lose track of: you're finding the things that you photograph often on a path that you take from one place to another within your life, regularly. I thought that was interesting because it incorporated chance, in a way, and routine—which is a form of pattern. So I'm intrigued to hear about that as well, but first talk about pattern.

MK: I've been making steel sculptures with woven lattices and Sheetrock wall drawings with different lattice patterns. I don't have a specific cultural reference for the simplified versions I use. I became interested in the lattice because it's familiar enough that one could recognize it from a garden or pattern in fabric, but also as a pattern that alludes to a structure that delineates and differentiates space; one that functions as both threshold and container. Also, the process of weaving makes the material stronger in steel or alludes to additional structural strength when depicted in Sheetrock.

I like what you said about the act of taking the photographs—it is a pattern. We live and work in New York, and I'm navigating places, which, for the most part, are gridded. The grid itself is a very specific pattern that's not so different from the lattice. For several years now, you've made photographic and sculptural representations of various cities. Neither of us have photojournalistic intentions, and your photographs tend to present the contours or textures of a place, so that its location can be accessed and felt. But you tend to work on location and not in New York.

SV: I have a really hard time shooting in New York. When I go to another city, I have this shifting engagement with it. Through photographing it I'm becoming familiarized with it, but I also remain an outside observer. So I have this push-pull relationship with my experience of the place that I enjoy. And I think that's why I've struggled with New York. At this point, even though I'm not from here, it's familiar. But that's why I love the images that you have taken here because the subjects are at times familiar, and through your compositional choices, your reorientation of the subject, or its combination with silk screen, the final works become these compelling abstract excerpts cut from a larger whole to exist in a new form that is unique unto itself, yet remains resonant of its original context.

This idea of cutting makes me want to return to pattern for a moment and discuss your works that involve incising drywall. Sheetrock is a construction-grade material, a module upon which much of our sense of contemporary

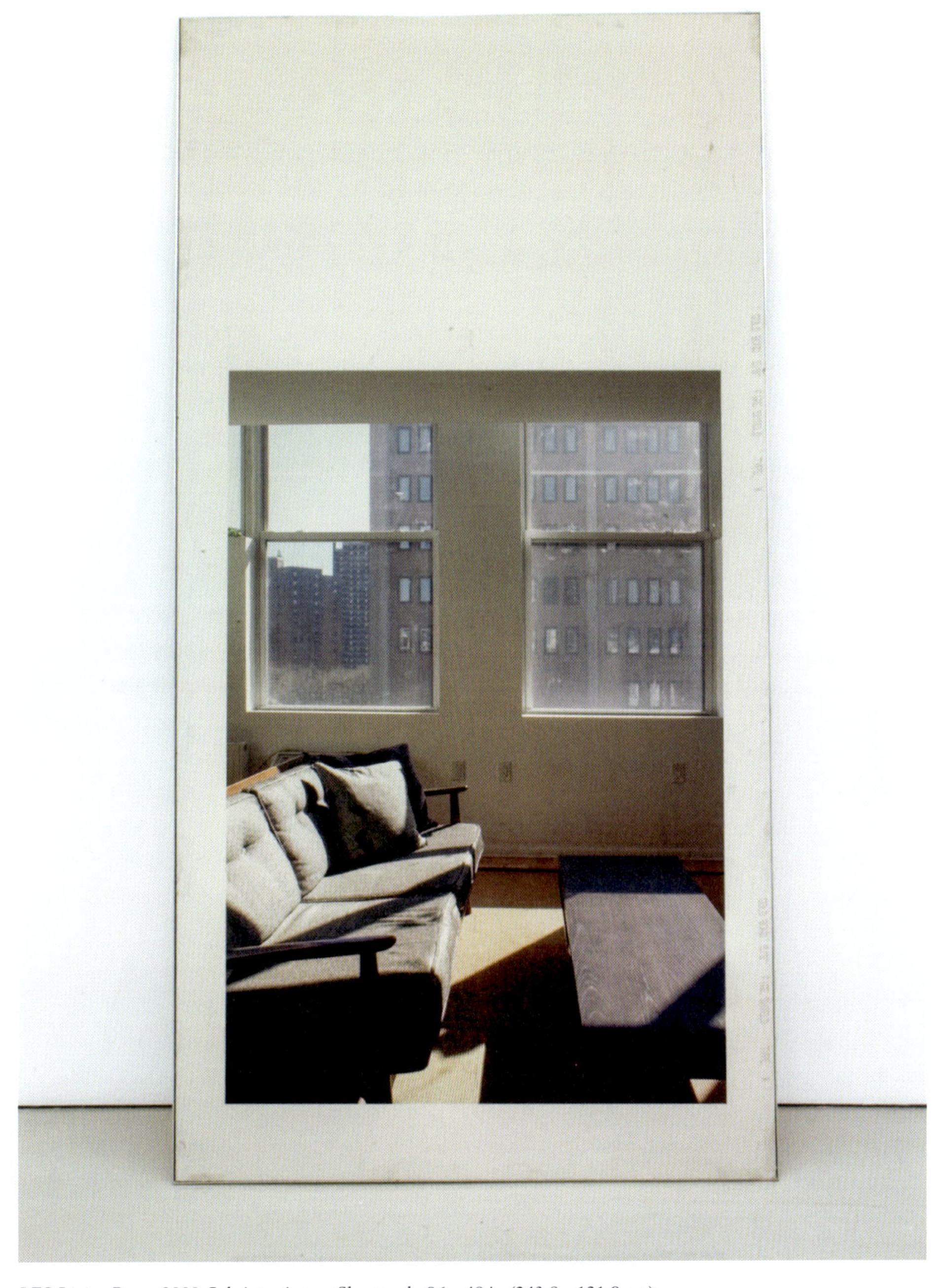

LES Living Room, 2009. Ink-jet print on Sheetrock. 96 x 48 in (243.8 x 121.9 cm).

space is formed, yet through this action of delineating pattern via your cutting, removing, or sanding elements of the Sheetrock, you create a shallow relief of sorts that equally embraces and disrupts our understanding of this ubiquitous material. But, importantly, the relief is created by hand. And with that, it also presents a use of the body and a mapping of space with the body that is important to talk about.

MK: When I started working with Sheetrock in grad school, I was drawn to its cheap price—it's ten dollars a sheet, it has a relationship to paper and the body, and we can understand it as part of most rooms. I do think that because I hand cut the Sheetrock patterns, it draws the viewer in at a different speed. I'm not interested in fetishizing that hand labor, but I am interested in creating a space that feels physically handled.

SV: The time-intensive or endurance discussion that comes along with handwork and repetition masks or distracts from some of the other things that are going on with these works. It's a building material that's been taken apart and built back up. As an installation, it is this amazing hybrid of drawing, painting, sculpture, and performance.

MK: And to bring it back to photography, when I've fed a piece of Sheetrock through an ink-jet printer, the sheet has a direct relationship with the way a photograph depicts space. The printed sheet of drywall and the membrane of the film or photographic paper are these thin materials that flatten a space that is potentially cavernous. This connects to the collages that I made for the "New Windows" show at D'Amelio Terras, documenting my super repairing the windows and the Sheetrock around them in my old apartment, seeing his body straddle inside and outside the building. That threshold is so permeable and negligible. And Sheetrock is a layer of that stratum—between interior and exterior—that has a resonance with film *in* the camera, or a kind of internal mechanism that records the external.

SV: I thought of that show as existing in this fragile membrane between waking life and dream life, or consciousness and the subconscious. That place in between is something I think about when trying to resolve how the final installation of an exhibition operates. Can you tell me about how you reach the final installation of your work? We've talked about the elements of the installation individually, but we haven't spoken yet about the whole: Do you sketch out your installations? Do you use a model? How do you go from the ideas and the discrete objects to the overall exhibition?

MK: I often like having a model around, and I've had foam-core models of galleries made. Using something like SketchUp just doesn't make sense to me, and floor plans don't make sense to me unless I need to understand how many sheets of Sheetrock or steel are required to tailor a space. But up to now, I walk around with a show in my head, and then there's usually a moment when something announces itself as a linchpin of sorts, and the installation will make sense to me.

SV: I love that you said you carry around the show in your head because that implies a physicality rather then a virtual rendering. There's clearly a great deal of consideration in advance on your part for the space in which the exhibition is occurring, yet at times you also seem to embrace moments of serendipity, both during your process of creating the works and within the final installation. I thought that was done really well in "I Apple New York." As a whole project, it contained various degrees of control. It was also like letting the universe in a little bit, too.

MK: That's part of what I love about photography. I love that it's evidentiary. It's not a facsimile of a thing in the world, and I don't want it to be. But I can cut away a portion of a location, photograph it with an incredible level of detail, and then insert it into a space that I'm creating. And by creating I mean, in the case of the Sheetrock or metal frieze for "I Apple New York," I'm developing a space and a display structure that the work resides within. That, to me, is important for the kind of mildly schizophrenic intentions of my work. As much as I love to make things, I also don't want to create an environment where the exterior world is erased from its inclusion.

I'm also interested in perception and phenomenology. I often take pictures of things that are on the ground and hang them vertically. And there's something immediately, physically understood when you look at a curb or a grate that's made vertical—you're understanding a shift between what's at your feet and your eyes, and the gravity of that. There's something I love about this, of reminding the viewer of the physical gravity of his or her body in the exhibition space, then underscoring that experience with the ocular activity that is looking at art.

SV: What you are saying about the exterior world is important. I think it's about striking a balance of intentionality and openness. It is important that an exhibition isn't so overtly considered that it sits in a vacuum, divorced from any sense of the larger world. And I think that the shows you have created are incredibly effective as an exhibition and as an experience because of this balance that you achieve with your work. Your work speaks to civic life, dream life, the internal life of an individual, but it also evaluates perception and phenomenology as well as various other formal concerns. Equally, there is a sense of gravity, a sense of

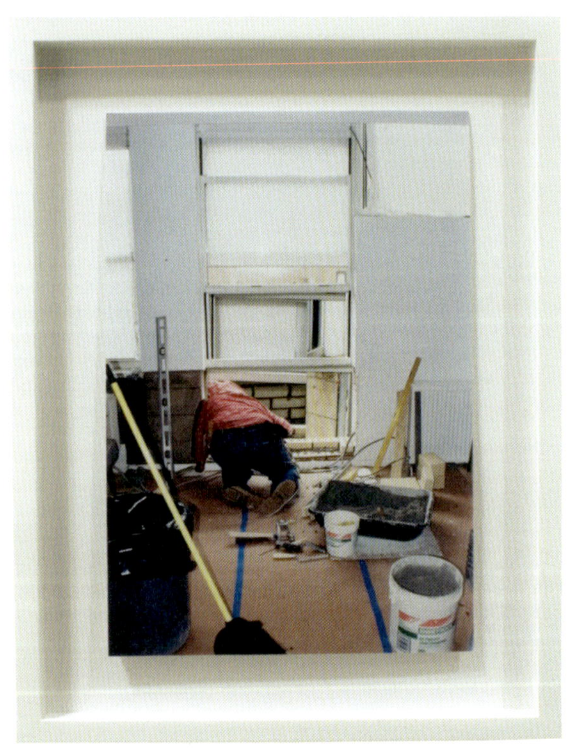

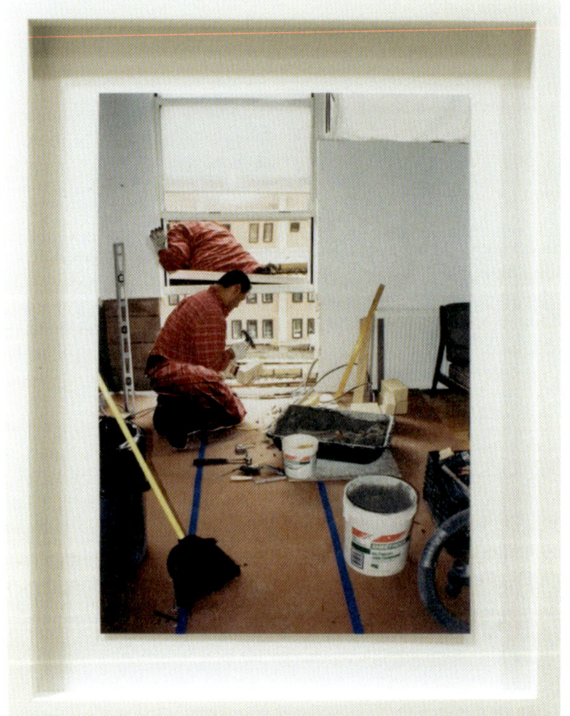

New Windows (#2–5), 2008. Collaged c-prints. 12 x 8 in (30.5 x 20.3 cm).

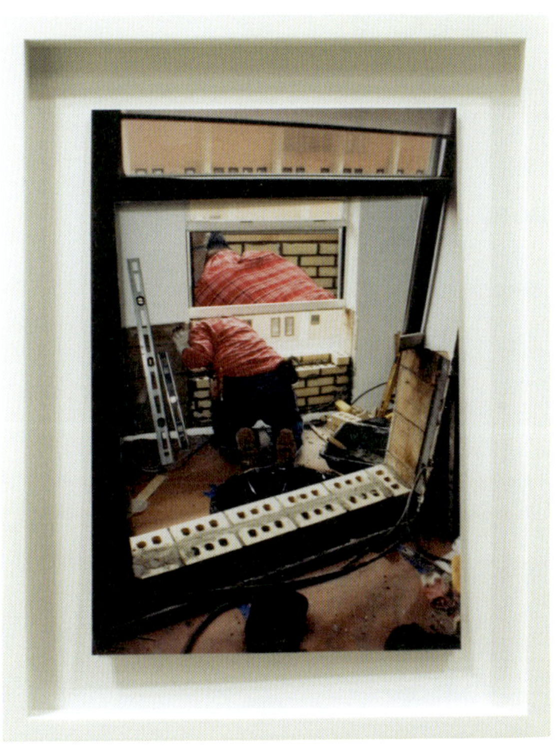

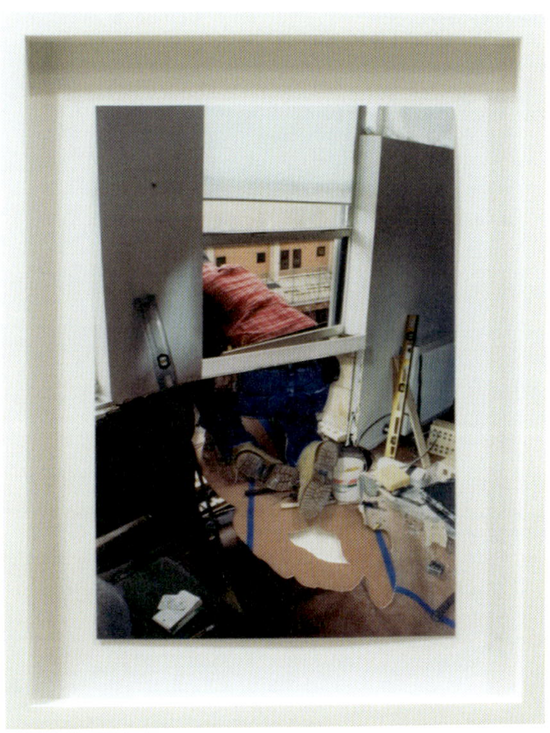

More Like, 2012. Latex paint on wall. Dimensions variable.

the body, and a sense of the places that we navigate every day. But because of the way in which you execute your work and arrange it in the space, it becomes something more—it is like a physical manifestation of the imagination and/or a concretization of the way we organize and process experience.

With this, I would imagine editing comes in somewhere to reach this effective balance that I see in your shows. Are you editing throughout the process of creation and then also during the final installation? Or, given that you work with fabricators on certain works, are you editing and focusing your idea prior to realizing the work?

MK: I'm glad you think editing is something I'm good at, because I have a tendency to overhang shows. I get excited to include a lot of things, and in retrospect I feel like my shows are trying to do too much. I definitely figure out a lot while installing the work, and I make more than I will need to be able to play around and swap out work. The overall installation structure and design is determined beforehand, but the actual order and hang is never fixed. There's no substitute for spending time in the space.

SV: Back to something you said earlier that I want you to expand on: the pattern of language. Language has been important to you in your work from very early on. You have used it for its meaning and its form. Letters and words have become modules at times in your installations. Do you look at a lot of poetry? Or are you thinking more about vernacular language and gleaning words or phrases from your life?

MK: I think it's a gleaning. In reading Eileen Myles or Anne Carson, the economy of their language resonates with me. I tend to be drawn to phrases and language that don't have flourish. I'm interested in the vernacular but also in breaking down phrases to their foundational architecture. "More Like Mother, More Like Father" is a good example. I'm drawn to phrases that have an implicit architecture and, often, symmetry. I made drawings, collages, and monoprints with the phrase "work from home." For the series *Work From Home*, all three words have the same number of letters; when stacked, a central "OR" snakes through.

SV: Do you consider the shapes of the letters themselves when thinking about pattern? I've been reading E. E. Cummings's poems recently, which is why I asked about poetry. I love Anne Carson, too. But what I really love about Cummings's work is when he starts to work with the shapes of the letters and the words, mixed with the sound and meaning of those words. I was thinking concrete. I think some of your works are like concrete poetry.

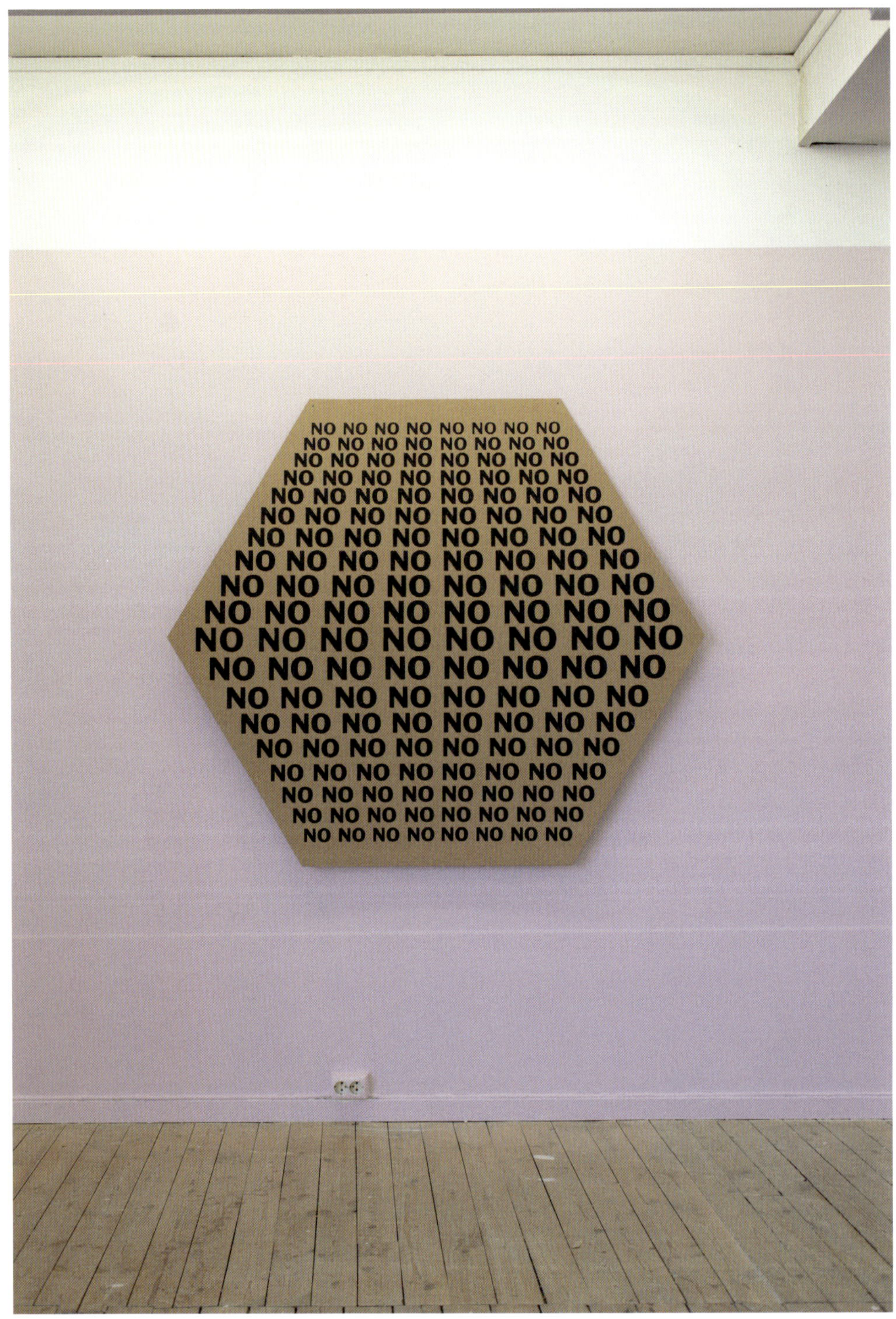

Installation view, 2015. "Portable Document Format," Rogaland Kunstsenter, Stavanger, Norway.

WORK FROM HOME

MK: I need to read Cummings! The poetry portion of the Carl Andre show at Dia:Beacon seems connected to what you're describing. It made so much sense to me because the arrangement of words and language on the page is *directly* translatable to how he arranges bricks or the tiles or the scattered sculptures. I *viscerally* relate to that use of language and think about that kind of building, construction, as being translatable to objects and things in the world.

My interest in language and translation connects to the fact that I grew up in a bilingual household but am not a fluent Spanish speaker, and grew up with the sound and rhythm of this other language. I always loved the awkward translations that my Cuban grandmother would say. And—totally off-track from Andre—when I graduated from undergrad she commended me for my work, and I said, tongue-in-cheek, perhaps as a provocation, that I was lucky. She said, "Luck nothing, you worked your ass out." [Laughs] Which of course, as a gay man, I thought was really funny. Because I was like, *What do you know?* [Laughs]

SV: That's great. Like your grandmother—you're taking something that's recognizable, but with your selection and repetition of it, it is transformed.
I think gaps in translation are fascinating, whether it's a bilingual household or Anne Carson translating ancient Greek poetry to modern English. This gets back to the sense of a liminal space. I enjoyed when you talked about language being this architecture, too, because with that idea I realize how much of our life is involved in creating and processing communication. Among all of our digital connectivity, gaps in comprehension along with moments of translation and mistranslation make it glaringly apparent that the membrane between connectivity, understanding, and complete disconnect is very thin.

MK: Language is this incredible thing because it is concrete and it does literally build space, and we could think about that in terms of its myriad bureaucratic functions. But, more interestingly, when there's fluency there is the ability to express oneself and connect, and almost merge with someone. There's an erotics to that.

SV: The merging of individuals causes me to return to where we began, discussing the mirror as a surface and a metaphor. I took it and the reflection it implies as a stand-in for images and the continual shifting sense of space, perception, time, and scale that can exist within a photograph.

MK: Yes—and, as you highlighted, this includes pattern and liminal space when taking photographs. Because I love problem-solving through language, it's taken me time to have faith in my materials to speak for me, so I also want to translate fluency to the process of making and editing.

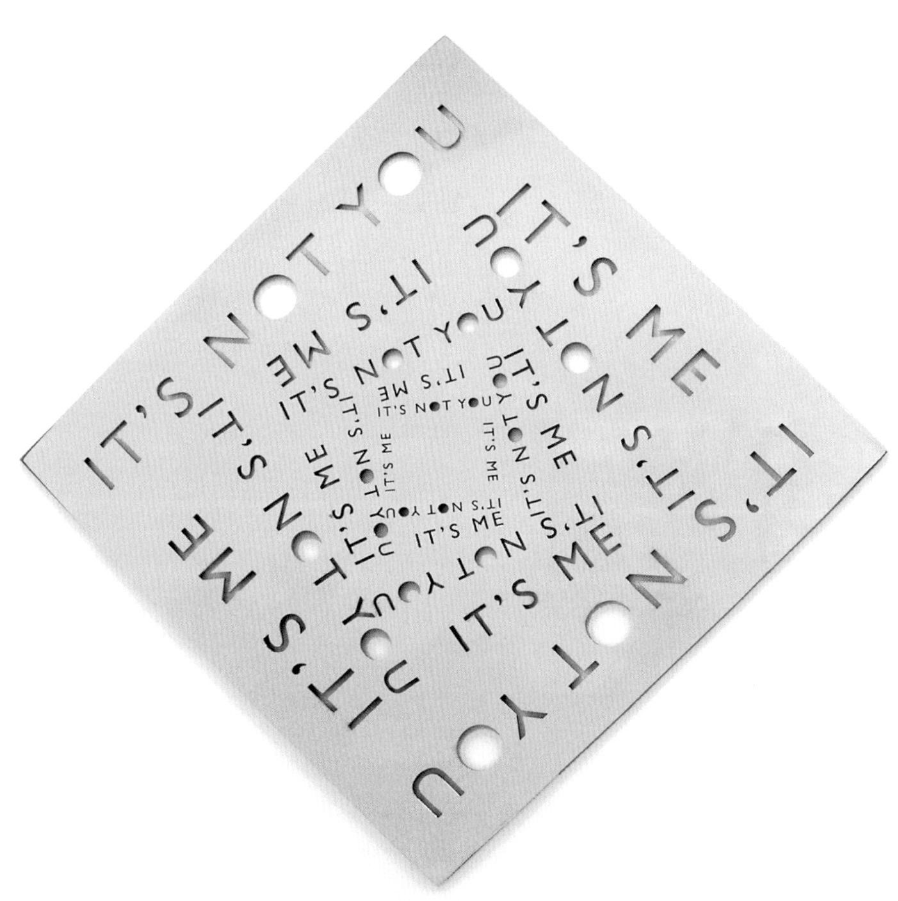

It's Not You, It's Me, 2011 Laser cut mirror-polished steel. 30 x 30 in (76.2 x 76.2 cm).

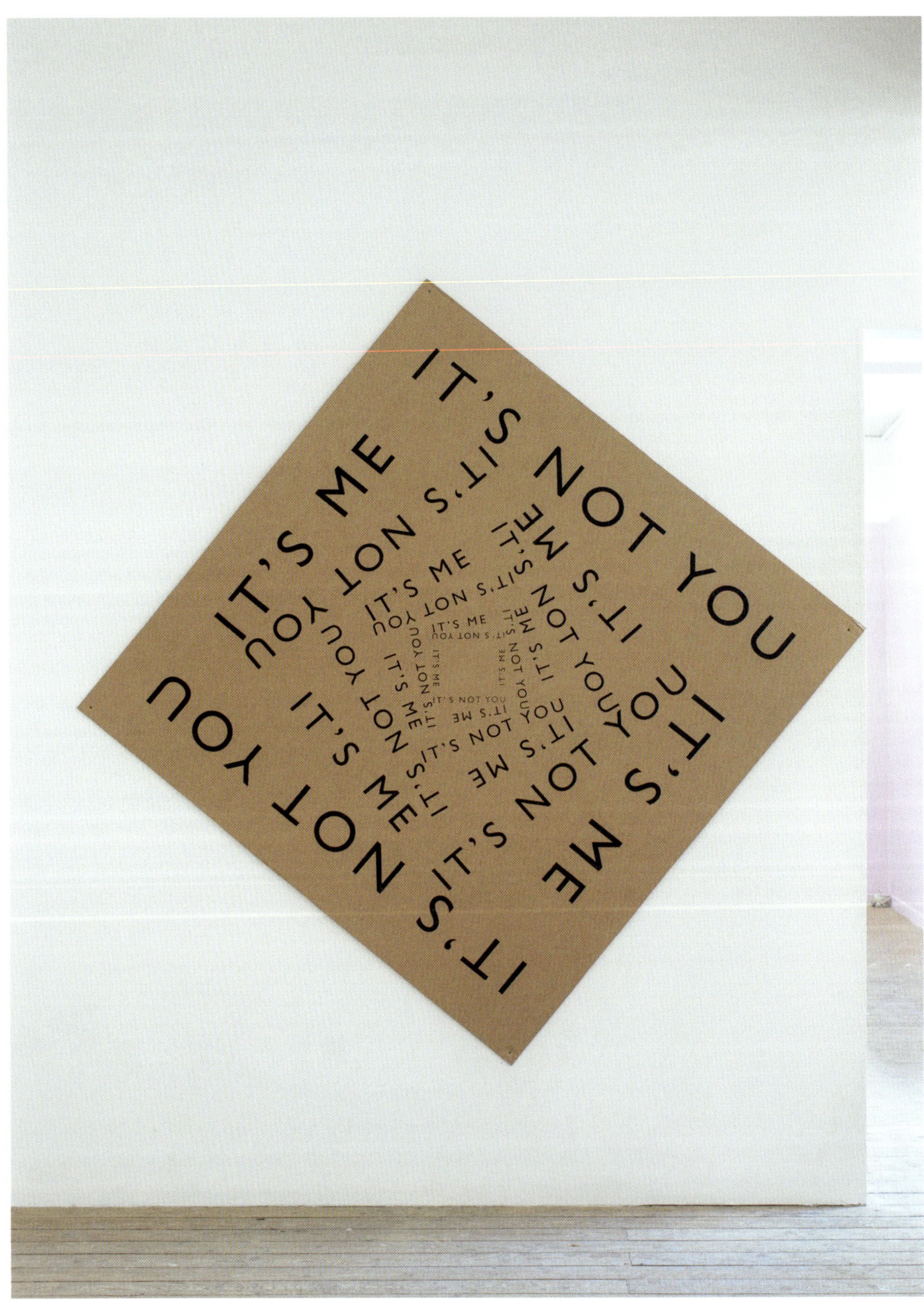

Installation view, 2015. "Portable Document Format," Rogaland Kunstsenter, Stavanger, Norway.

PRACTICE, PRACTICE, PRACTICE

A Conversation with Anna Craycroft

Anna Craycroft: In Tom McDonough's essay, in this catalogue, he describes your recent folded steel sculptures as *awaiting language*. I love the proposition inherent to this "pause"—a patient but direct request that isn't simply awaiting a title, which could be said of most abstraction. Their wait is for *language*—and as such they're inherently dialogic.

The importance of conversation and the conversational is an active element in all your work—and extends to how you approach exhibition making, programming, and publishing. For your recent show at Rogaland Kunstsenter in Stavanger, Norway, you remade a number of existing metal and Sheetrock text works in cardboard. Was this gesture an introduction to a new audience?

Matt Keegan: An introduction is a great way of framing this work and show. I selected sixteen sculptures originally made between 2006 and 2014, and remade them in double-wall cardboard at the Kunstsenter and print shop, located in the same building. I chose cardboard because I often figure out sculptures in this material, but also for its chameleon-like properties, its fidelity to Sheetrock and steel, and its ability to be easily disposed of.

I think of the cardboard versions as stand-ins, which doesn't make them lesser than the originals, but they're different. Their life is intertwined with the run of the show, called "Portable Document Format." People who worked on "PDF" get to choose a sculpture, and the rest gets recycled. Knowing this, I also chose cardboard because its color is close to a gray card, used to set light readings when taking photos. When the show is over, the work will only exist as photographs.

AC: I see a deliberate effort in your exhibitions to highlight a space outside the finite parameters of a single venue or moment, mostly through programmed events and related publications, but also very much in the individual objects and their installations.

MK: The original sculptures remade for "PDF" all began as some type of file format, and they often started as printouts before becoming sculptures. This directly connects to their reproducibility and ease of circulation. I'm glad that this translates for you to my interest in publications, because the process of making and assembling these works bears a likeness to the production of an edition.

I'm interested in how work can be reconfigured, recontextualized, and reevaluated in the midst of an exhibition, and programming can help do that. Your recent show, "C'mon Language," [at the Portland Institute for Contemporary Art in Oregon, in summer 2013] is a great, sort of extreme version of this. You invited me to program an afternoon event, and I was able to see firsthand how you successfully created a show that did not have a central artwork or installation around which the programming happened, so the show was perpetually in formation.

AC: Perpetually, so it was difficult to measure *anything*, especially success! [Laughs] The installation that I designed to house and facilitate the events was in constant flux. At the entrance to the show there was a wall text that read as the tenet of the exhibition: how do we make ourselves understood? And because the show was situated within an art institution, the question was *also* about how an artwork is being understood. For me, the question was a direct link between art and pedagogy, which I consider to be deeply interconnected. I see programming as a way to engage others—audiences, contributors, collaborators—in a question that I have been asking alone in the studio. So there is an aspiration for a progression of logic or meaning. My interest in the social is very much about a desire to explore topics in real time with others: How do languages form? What does learning look like? When is an artwork transformative? Questions you can't really answer on your own. Embedding programming within an exhibition is a way to admit to the chaos behind this seemingly resolved installation—and to open up the possibility that new connections can be made—to keep the project from concluding in a single, solitary moment of clarity.

But your approach to programming feels more temperate. In your practice the conversational feels like a series of reflections, or radial relationships. I experience the social components of your work as discreet spaces that reflect and echo each other. And I see you as deliberately allowing for this to take place in unexpected or unintended ways.

MK: Is there a particular project that you're thinking of?

AC: One anecdote that comes to mind took place when the third edition of *North Drive Press* was about to be released. Many of us who made works or interviews for the publication came together to help assemble the boxes. Just by standing next to one another as we compiled the various parts and pages, editions in various media, we began talking about what we were looking at. We

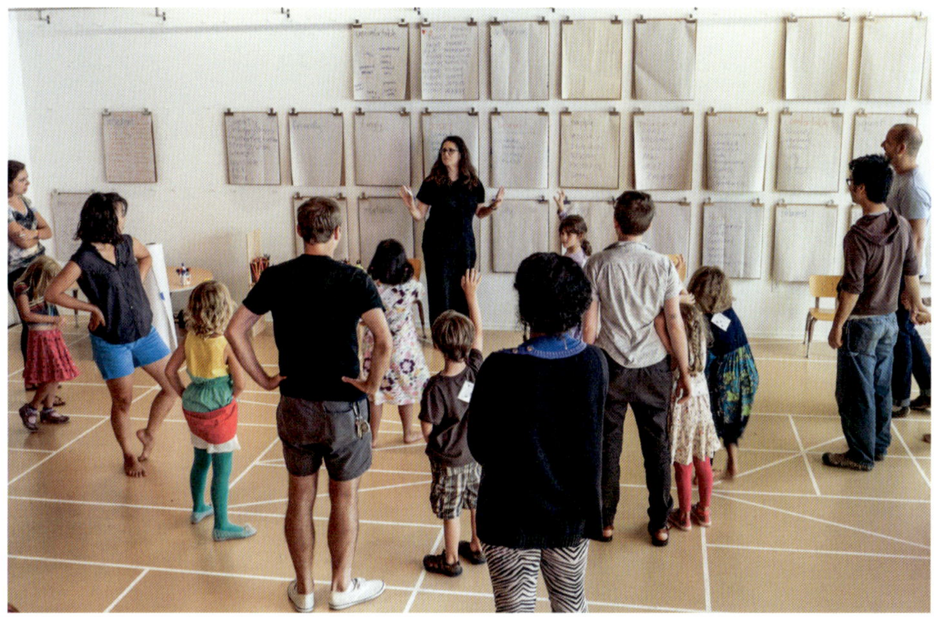

Anna Craycroft, Installation view, 2013. *C'mon Language*, Portland Institute for Contemporary Art, Portland, OR.

had each put a lot of thought and work into our contributions, so the conversations could get quite in-depth and specific. At the same time they were discrete and casual. I think this is due to how you bring people together. It's kind of an organized informality, and it breeds very open dialogue that allows each participant to maintain his or her own space, interests, and voice.

For me, this is an example of how your publications and exhibitions seem to pose a simple but difficult question: How do you get a bunch of people into a space where *real* conversations can happen? Not "lessons" or solutions, but social engagements where an experience is shared, and the outcome is not predetermined. Maybe this gets back to that "pause" I was talking about earlier—that space that provides room and doesn't force things to fit together.

MK: I'm invested in the productive space of conversation and meandering discussion. *North Drive Press* (www.northdrivepress.com) directly grew out of the highly discursive MFA program that we both attended at Columbia University. That immersion in rich and generative dialogue made me want to create a publishing platform that featured artist-to-artist interviews between mainly "emerging" practitioners. As a collection of five issues made over the course of six years, *NDP*'s interviews are rich in intimate dialogues on personal practice more than traditional

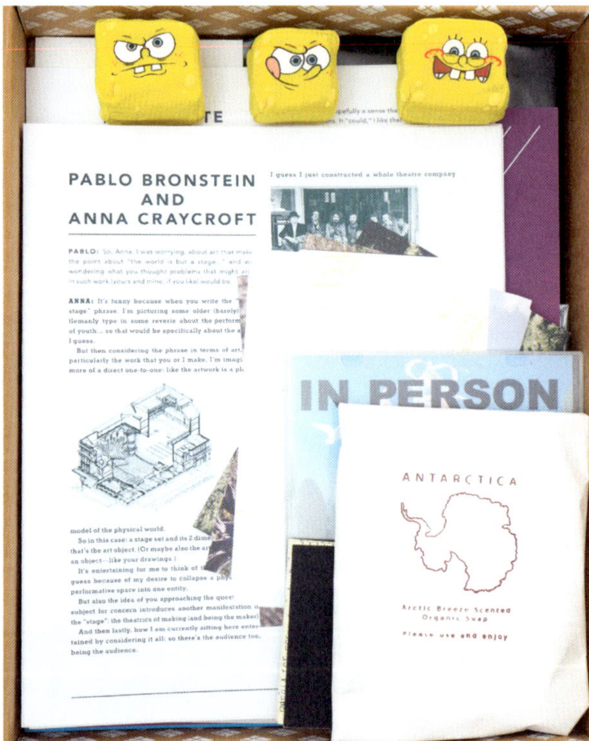

North Drive Press #3, 2006. Sara Greenberger Rafferty co-editor. North Drive Press #5, 2010 both in an edition of 500. Collected interviews, texts, and multiples. Su Barber, art director for both issues.

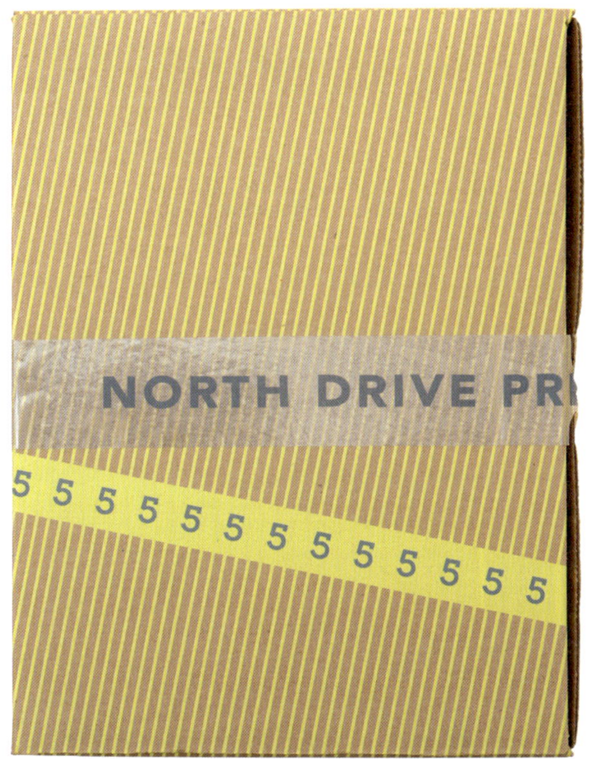
NORTH DRIVE
5 5 5 5 5 5 5 5 5 5 5 5 5

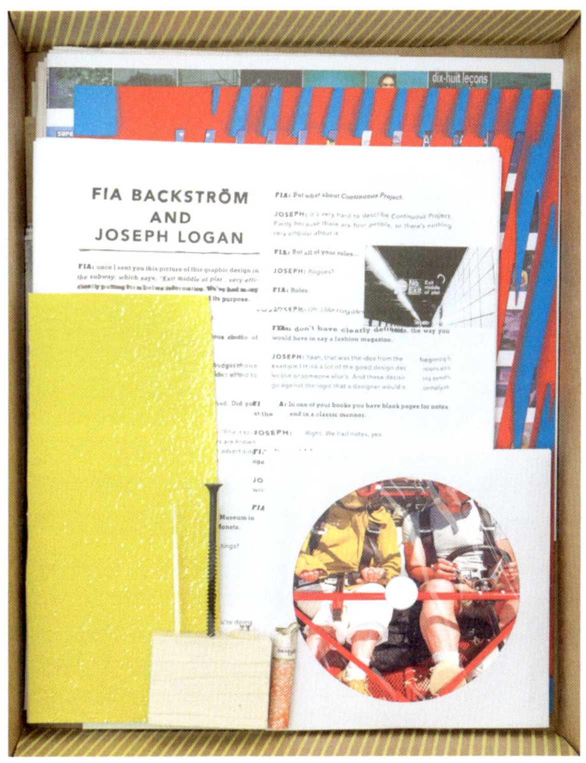
dix-huit leçons
FIA BACKSTRÖM
AND
JOSEPH LOGAN

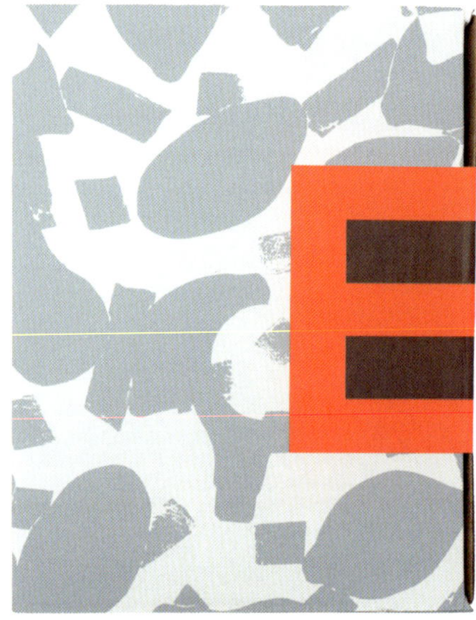

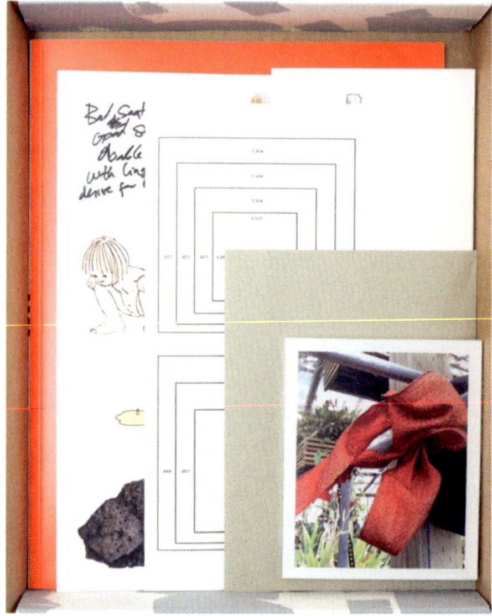

==#2, 2015. Published by Capricious, Su Barber, art director. Edition of 500.

scholarship, but I was and am interested in creating a space for conversation that isn't always conclusive. This has continued with == (www.equalequal.info).

AC: It seems like the finite nature of a publication or exhibition would make it impossible to "go on record" in an inconclusive way. How can you undo this fixed form and the expectations that come with it?

MK: *NDP* and == are both non-thematic publications, and this allows for a variety of topics to cohabitate within each issue. Ideally this has a closer relationship to ongoing dialogues—yes, they're conclusive because they're printed and there's an end, but the interviews that are especially good feel like they're excerpted from ever-evolving discussions.

In terms of exhibition, I think the related publication is the best way to extend its life, and I treat it as its own site—rather than a catalogue—that reads as a record of something that happened.

AC: The publications that you make in relation to your exhibition—I'm thinking specifically of *AMERICAMERICA*—take your research and represent it in a new form, and in this way are works in and of themselves. In some cases they also exist within the exhibition. But you were also talking about *NDP* and ==, which are not related to a given exhibition.

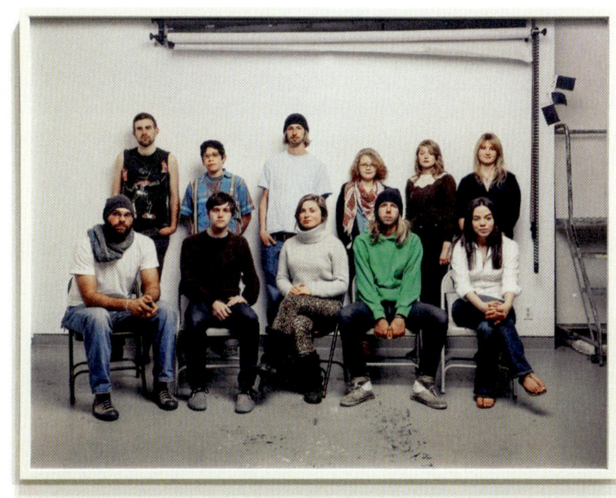

Mondays 9–3pm, 2009. C-print. 30 x 37¾ in (76.2 x 95.9 cm).

For a while you were regularly involved in projects, curating group shows, organizing panels, and publications that were not connected to exhibitions of your own. More recently you have been making that collective space more centrally located in your work. At what point did you begin bringing that programming *within* your practice?

MK: Well, I didn't do any programming in conjunction with "Any Day Now," which was my first solo show [in September 2007 at D'Amelio Terras, New York]. I had just come off of *a lot* of organizational work. I had cocurated [with Rachel Foullon and Laura Kleger as Public-Holiday Projects] "Bunch Alliance and Dissolve," which included your work and was a twenty-seven-person show at the Contemporary Arts Center in Cincinnati in fall 2006. The year before I had organized six months of programming, including two group shows as part of a project called *Etc.*, at a temporary space run by Andrew Kreps. Additionally, I had worked on three issues of *North Drive Press* by that point. But, between 2008 and 2012, my solo shows always included some form of programming.

For "Now's the Time," at Anna Helwing Gallery, Los Angeles, in 2008, I included a variety of events.

AC: And how did that come about?

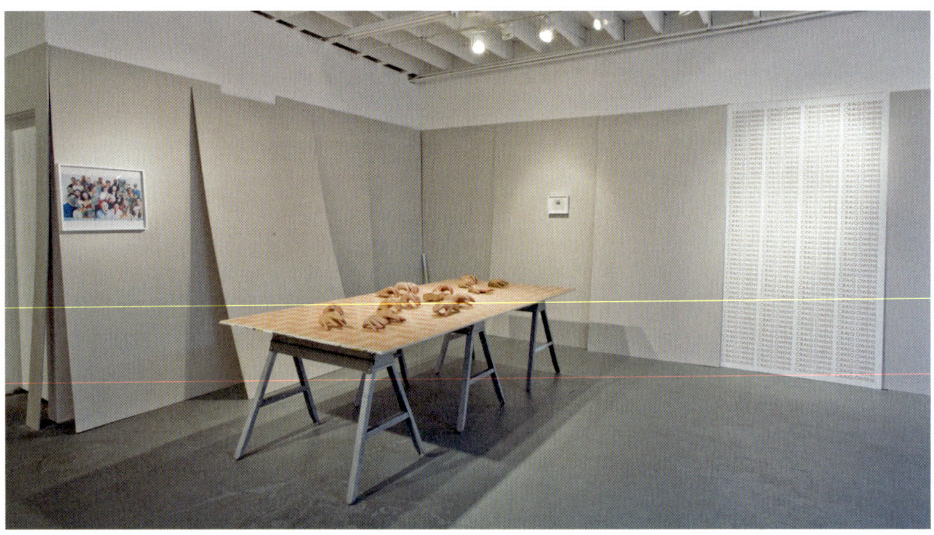

Installation View, 2008. "Now's the Time," Anna Helwing Gallery, Los Angeles, CA.

MK: "Now's the Time" was made in conjunction with *AMERICAMERICA*, which was an artist book commissioned by Printed Matter. Both exhibition and book looked at points of overlap between the lead-up to the 2008 US presidential election and the year 1986, toward the end of Reagan's second term as president.

Hands Across America functioned as a point of departure for the whole project. HAA was a fundraiser held on May 25, 1986, to benefit America's homeless population. People joined hands between Battery Park City, New York, and Long Beach, California—including President Reagan and the first lady—on that day in solidarity for the cause. Never mind that Reagan was directly responsible for dismantling social programming within this country or that the very belated and public discussion of AIDS and the *Bowers versus Hardwick* ruling were also at this time. This physical linkage across the country seems bizarre and delusional in relation to these facts. In the lead-up to 2008's election, we understood our country as being fractured into red and blue states, making it impossible to imagine people joining hands between the coasts for a shared cause.

The programming for "Now's the Time" looked at the cultural moment of the mid to late 1980s through music—mixtapes and 'zines, performance, and independent filmmaking—to highlight forgotten recent history and to mine places of repetition.

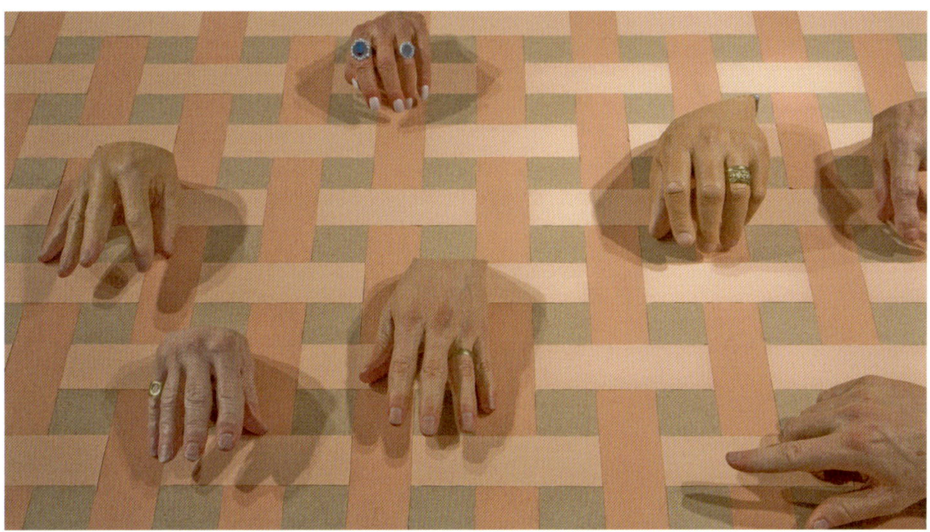

Hands Almost Across America (New York - New Mexico), 2008. Acrylic paint on Sheetrock, acrylic on 15 hydrocal casts, and metal saw horses. 29¼ x 96 x 48 in (74.3 x 243.8 x 121.9 cm).

AC: Can you describe how the programming physically fit within your installation?

MK: That was the first time that I made an installation comprised of loose, leaning panels of Sheetrock, a material I began working with while in grad school. The sheets featured hand-cut patterns and text that were incised and sometimes painted. The installation had the ability to be easily reconfigured to suit the needs of screenings, panel discussions, or otherwise.

AC: So would you say that the screenings, panel discussions, and such were a way to materialize the research so that it was on par with the physical installation?

MK: Yeah, you can think of it that way.

AC: But I want to be clear that I'm not considering your research as an explanatory or didactical backstory. I'm visualizing your research-to-programming as a mirroring of processes. It makes sense to me that it should be as actively present in the space of the exhibition as, say, your Sheetrock installation.

MK: Your question reminds me of how directly informed "Now's the Time" was by making *North Drive Press*. I began to think about the gallery as a box

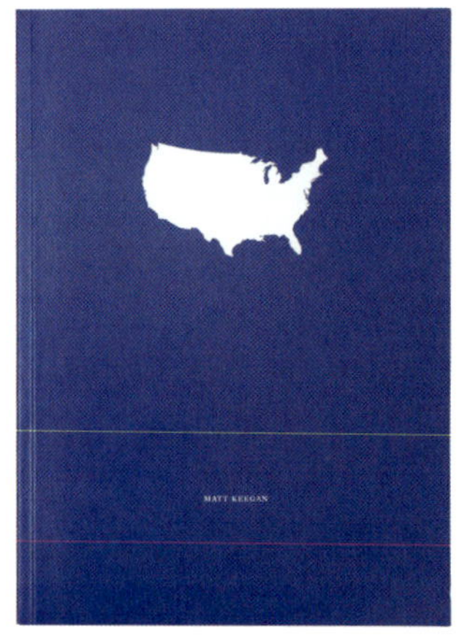

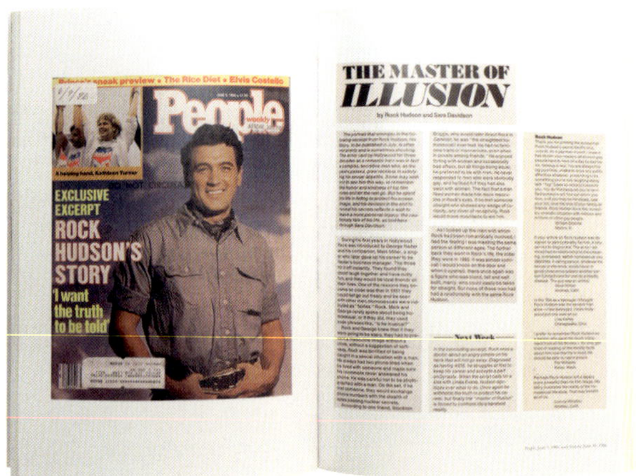

AMERICAMERICA, 2008. Commissioned by Printed Matter, New York, NY.

that's reconfigurable, like that publication. In 2008 this was obviously not a new thought, but it was very freeing and exciting to make this connection between these two projects. And back to your comment about research—we both love the process of translating and integrating research into exhibitions, but neither of us are interested in providing the finite guiding voice. This seems important to highlight in relation to the idea of something being or remaining in flux.

AC: Yes, one of the things I love about both *NDP* and == is the design by Su Barber. The box is such a casual frame—barely there, so that the contents really stand out as discrete thoughts that each belong to a different source. Within my exhibitions, when I invite people to lead workshops or performances, I also make an effort to give them the center stage and spotlight. But my frame is *way* less casual—the umbrella concept or physical platform of the installation is always present, either in the way the show has been programmed, or with the space they are asked to work within. It is important to me to maintain some presence.

MK: I do think that's something that differentiates us—I think of you more as a director or ringleader, whereas I definitely prefer to be behind the scenes.

AC: That's true, but I think of each of your shows as starting from a specific point of intimacy. When you put a show together and connect disparate parts, there's a source you begin with that is deeply felt—whether that source is related

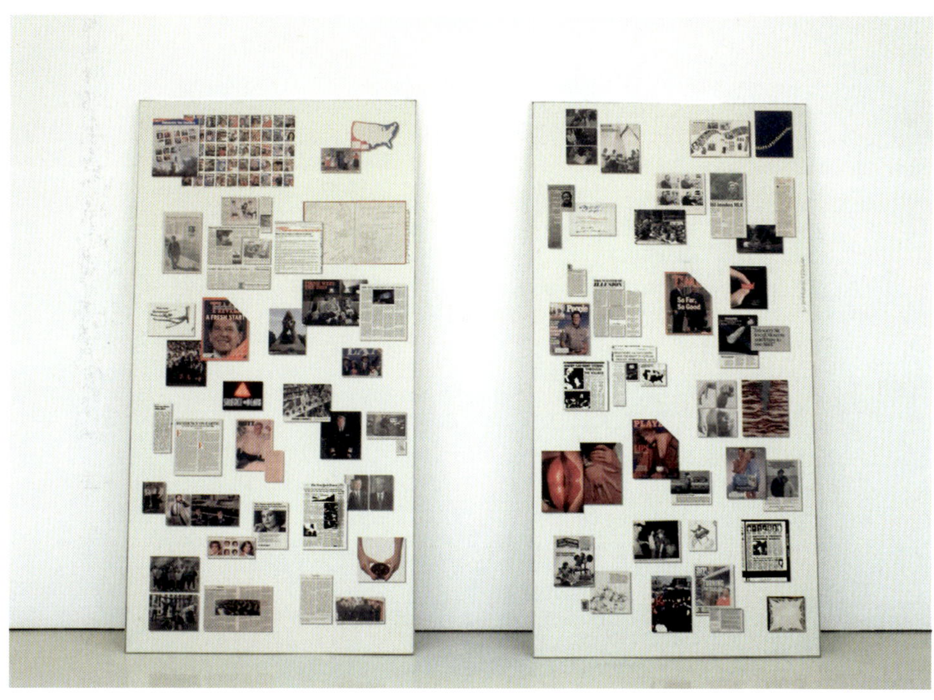

AMERICAMERICA excerpt #1 & excerpt #2, 2009. Ink-jet prints on Sheetrock. 96 x 48 in (243.8 x 121.9 cm) each.

to friends, lovers, family, someone you revere, or another person who becomes the subject of the exhibition. This intimate beginning sets a precedent: you're making something that you care about, including other people, and within the exhibition you reveal these personal, shared moments.

I'm remembering specifically two photos in "I Apple NY" that you shot spontaneously on a walk you and I took together. We were meandering through the West Village one spring afternoon and suddenly you were marveling at the noxious pink villa where Julian Schnabel lives, framed by the Westbeth Artists Housing in the foreground, just around the corner from the Jane Jacobs housing complex. Because we had both been New York City kids, the years of our childhood—the '70s, '80s, '90s—were spelled out in these architectural adjacencies, which really resonated for both of us. Plus this sequence of buildings linked all these books you were reading and people you were talking to in preparation for your upcoming show.

You translated the intimacy of that moment and its connection to a larger political infrastructure by simply affixing the modest photos with magnets to a large sheet of painted steel. In this way many of the photos in the show seemed like footnotes or personal associations that had to have come from moments

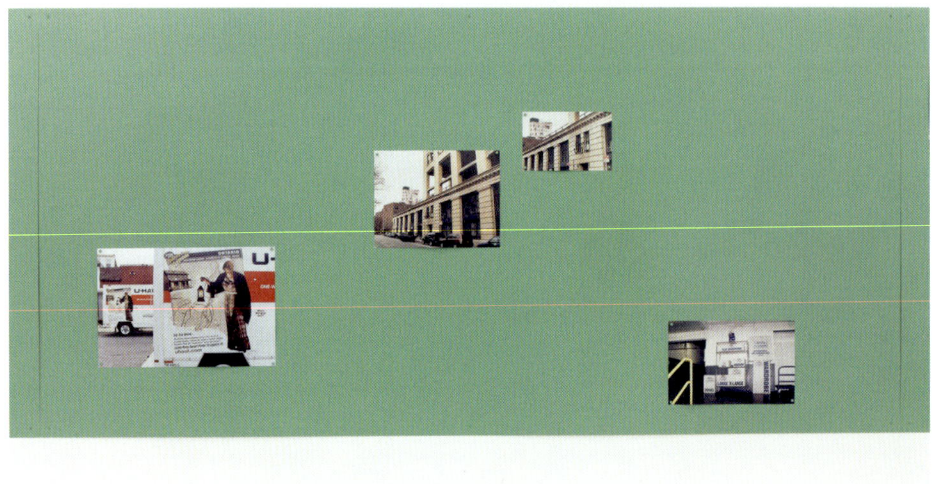

Untitled (Group 12), 2011. Four c-prints attached with magnets to steel panels spray-finished in Aluminum Green. 48 x 96 in (121.9 x 243.8 cm).

like the one we shared. It's the allusion to intimacies like these that make me wonder about how your exhibitions originate. Can you talk a little about where you begin?

MK: How they start is contingent on each exhibition. Over the last four years, a more project-based approach has been sidestepped for a more material-based exploration. I gave a lecture at NYU in 2012 and spoke about "I Apple New York," the show that contained the photos of Schnabel's Palazzo Chupi and Westbeth, and "Lengua," an exhibition mainly comprised of the laser-cut steel sculptures, both mounted in 2011. I found that I was able to speak about them clearly, and was pleased with the talk, but afterward I felt like something was wrong with the fact that I could speak about the work so conclusively.

The following year, I began to archive my work from undergrad up to when I started exhibiting after grad school, and I was reminded of my emphasis on making and understanding decisions through making things—working with one material over another based on a specific project and not wanting language or a project-based approach to neutralize or homogenize that.

AC: Such a nice proposition. If the material is "doing the talking," we can't be sure that we know what it's saying. I love your video *"N" as in Nancy* (www.mattkeegan.info/index.php?/ma/ma/) because it asks this question of understanding even within language itself. For me that video is this beautiful play with the function of the didactic—which is one place where I think art and pedagogy overlap. Watching the video feels like a proposition that *anything*—object, event, exhibition, classroom, etc., can be a teaching tool. And most significantly, what *"N" as in Nancy* demonstrates is that as a "teaching tool," or artwork, it is an opportunity for invention—a dynamic and nonhierarchical learning space.

MK: It makes sense that you'd respond to *"N" as in Nancy* as it's my artwork that most explicitly connects with the expansive potential of pedagogy. And I like that you connect this question of how we read a photograph or a sculpture with this video. With my new steel sculptures that don't have text, I love that they still illicit a reading, meaning when people look at them they immediately say, "That looks like armor," or "It looks like a mask."

AC: Yes, I love that about those sculptures. But especially how they do this through process. The slight bending and weaving of their flat forms read like playful but poignant moments of stopping. As though in the middle of a process of discovery—folding, cutting, opening, etc.—the activity was halted. In this way the sculptures feel like teaching tools. Similar to how you present your mother's ESL flash cards in *"N" as in Nancy*, they lay bare the open-endedness of learning.

MK: I also see a relationship with reading the shapes and the stock images that my mother used to teach English—though we may be alone in this! [Laughs] The shapes with laser-cut text take on the voice of a dry narrator and in some cases are instructional, while, as you mentioned, the shapes that are absent of language function more as icons that I could see being used as learning aids.

AC: Earlier, I said that I think art and pedagogy are deeply interwoven. From this perspective we could say that the exhibition itself acts as an instructor in the absence of the artist. The exhibition reveals or withholds the learning process that has been inherent to the evolution of the artwork for the artist. When presenting the outcome of this process, the artist has a choice as to whether his or her exhibition "instructs" in an open-ended way—putting the agency for learning in the hands of the audience—or in a fixed or finite way, keeping the knowledge in the hands of the artist. I see the "hands off" approach that features in all your work—objects, events, exhibitions, publications, etc.—as a generous act of putting agency in the hands of the audience.

MK: That's good to hear! I am nervous to equate the exhibition with the voice of an instructor. Though I relate in terms of the way that I build out shows and think about how a viewer moves through them, and how to slow down that process. I still want that space to be more open, surprising, and even confusing. Recently, in my two-person show with Anne Truitt, my solo show "And," and in remaking sculptures for "PDF," I've let the physical making and selected material do more of the talking. This has felt destabilizing, because it's less conclusive, but it feels interconnected with the process of learning.

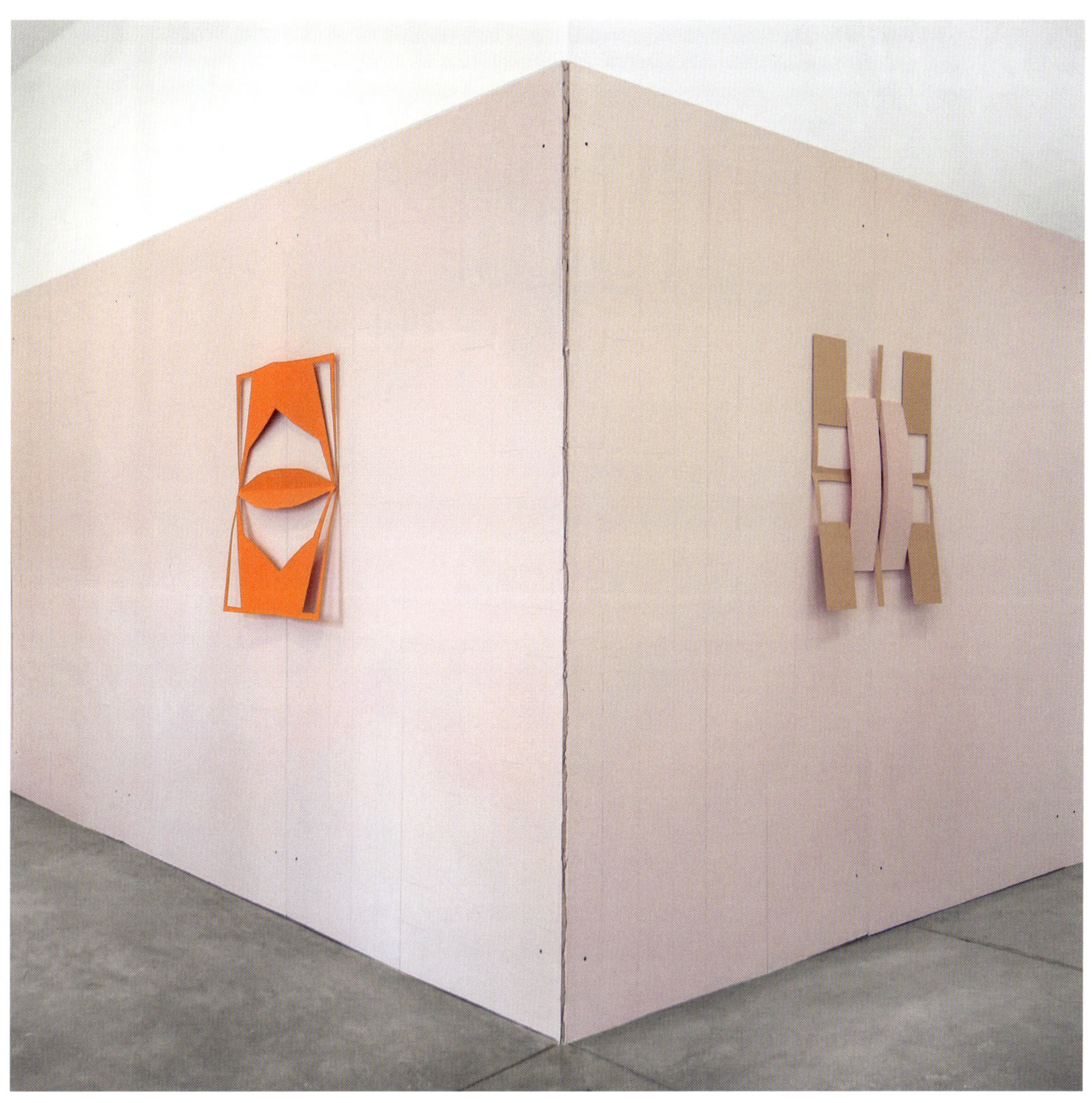

Installation view, 2015. “And,” Altman Siegel, San Francisco, CA.

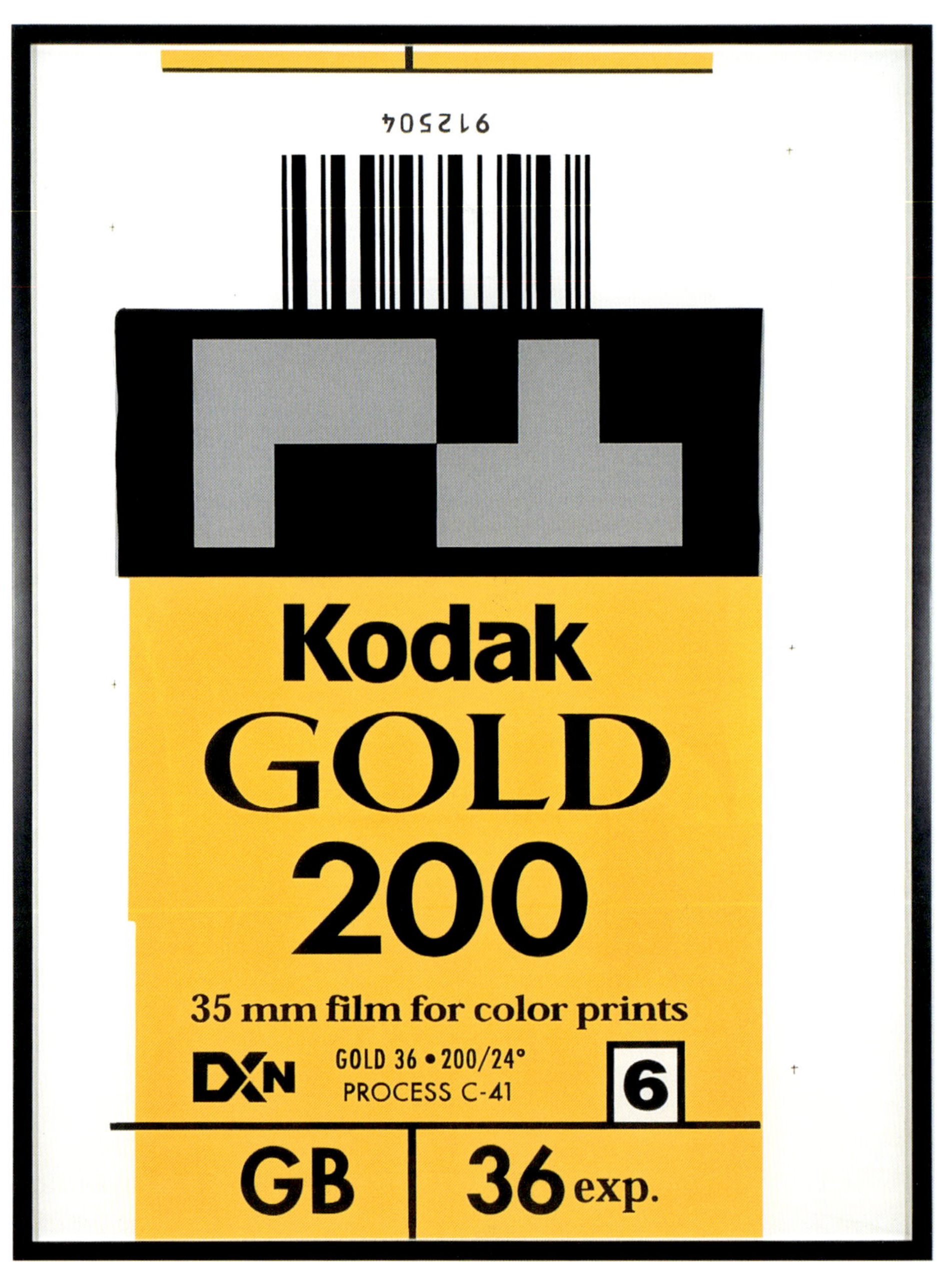

Kodak 200, 2006. Silkscreen on Coventry paper. 64 x 46 in (162.6 x 116.8 cm).

May 2015

Dear Matt,

I feel like much of our relationship as friends and artists exists within the realm of the personal. From our very first meeting, the assertion that "the personal" is a space upon which we connect and continue to connect with others was clearly established. Is this not what it means to be an artist who understands the paradigm shift from the twentieth century into the twenty-first? Are we (artists, citizens, human beings) connecting to one another? Or are we drifting apart, having less and less of a connection to the real world in favor of the virtual one? Below is a selection of passages from my private writing. Though we often do not address many of these concerns verbally, our works are always in dialogue, responding to the world we share, yet through distinct ways:

There is something strange that occurs when I travel without a camera. I ache. There is an empty feeling in the hollowed area of my chest after a deep breath. I yearn to capture, to hold still, that which is fleeting with the surety that I may investigate, relive, and explore the details of time partially experienced for the purpose of future-tense looking. This sensation is similar to what I imagine is at the heart of Walter Mischel's marshmallow experiment. This wanting to delay and defer with the hope that there is a similar yet distinctly different and more porous moment at the opposite end of the photographic engagement is a primal desire for me. Exchanging the actual moment for its simulacra, the preferred reward.

I too feel lost somehow, as if I am traveling without direction (without my camera). I am no longer surefooted. I don't know where to focus my gaze, other than to profess that I need evidence of today, tomorrow, and yesterday. My mind is not trustworthy. I change things and misremember them. It is more convenient to rely on the monocular lens, double vision centralized. Two forces like a father's sperm and a mother's egg, joining to create new life. Is that a strange analogy? I am sorry about that. What to do with this floating sensation? Where shall I go? What is its surrogate?

I recently found this image of a seascape (inserted here), which I took with my camera phone while traveling from Bodø to Svolvær, Norway, by boat in 2013. Think of the image as a kind of MTPE: memory travel postcard experiment, merging my desire to communicate with you through images over time and to somehow close the physical distance—and my lamenting of what to do with such feelings of longing.

Your friend,
Leslie

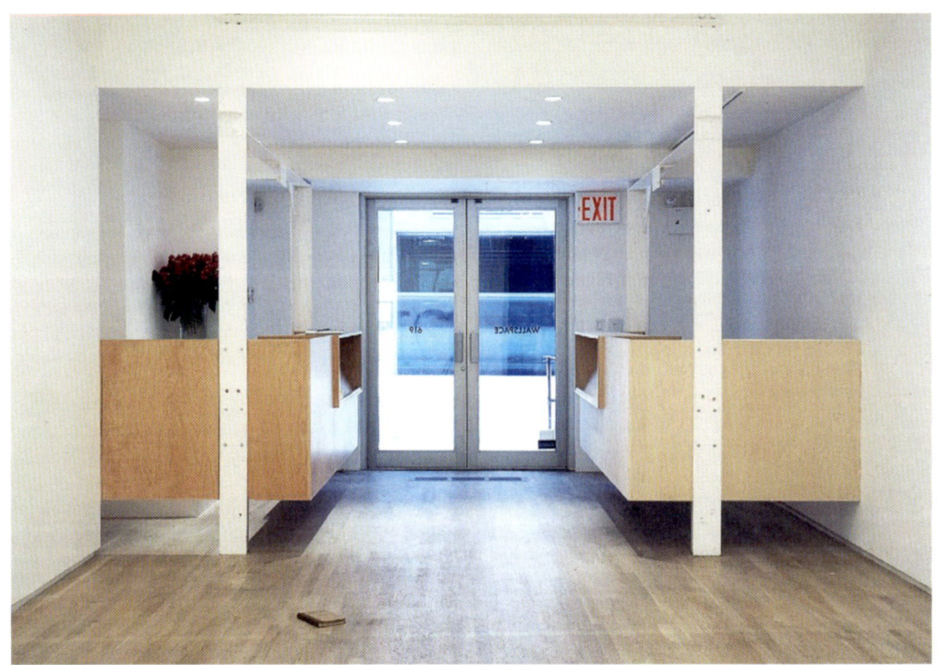

Installation view, 2006. "From You to Me and Back Again (Leslie Hewitt and Matt Keegan)" Wallspace Gallery, New York, NY.

BIOGRAPHY

Lives and works in Brooklyn, NY

Solo and Two-Person Exhibitions

2016
Two-person show with Kay Rosen, Grazer Kunstverein, Graz, Austria
"A Traveling Show," Matt Keegan and Kay Rosen, Contemporary Art Museum, Houston, TX

2015
"Portable Document Format," Rogaland Kunstcenter, Stavanger, Norway
"And," Altman Siegel, San Francisco, CA

2014
"Matt Keegan and Anne Truitt," Andrea Rosen Gallery 2, New York, NY

2013
"Horizon," Galeria Pedro Cera, Lisboa, Portugal

2012
"Y? O! G... A.," Matt Keegan and Eileen Quinlan, Curated by Matthew Lyons, The Kitchen, New York, NY
"Millennium Magazines," Museum of Modern Art, New York, February 20–May 14, 2012

2011
"Lengua," Altman Siegel, San Francisco, CA
"I Apple NY," D'Amelio Terras, New York, NY

2010
"The Story of a Window," with Dane Mitchell, Neon Parc, Melbourne, Australia

2009
"Postcards & Calendars," Altman Siegel Gallery, San Francisco, CA
"New Windows," D'Amelio Terras, New York, NY

2008
"Now's the Time," Anna Helwing Gallery, Los Angeles, CA

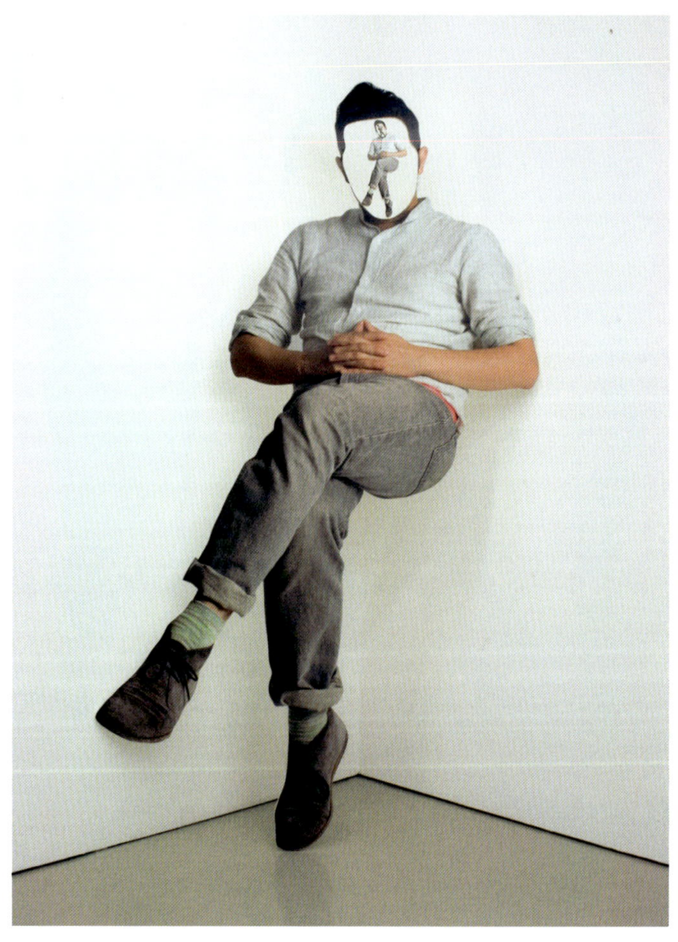

Humberto, Humberto, Humberto, 2007. 3 digital c-prints mounted on gatorboard 97 x 41 in (246.38 x 104.14 cm).

2007
"Any Day Now," D'Amelio Terras, New York, NY

2006
"From You to Me and Back Again" with Leslie Hewitt, Wallspace Gallery, New York, NY
"How to Make a Portrait," Nicole Klagsbrun, New York, NY and White Columns, New York, NY

Selected Group Shows

2015
"Reconstructions: Recent Photographs and Video from the Met Collection," Metropolitan Museum of Art, New York, NY
"Storylines: Contemporary Art at the Guggenheim," Solomon R. Guggenheim Museum, New York, NY
"Over & Under," Sikkema Jenkins & Co., New York, NY

2014
"Rencontre," Curated by Janneke deVries, Autocenter, Berlin, Germany
"No Games Inside the Labyrinth," Curated by John Miller, Galerie Barbara Weiss, Berlin, Germany
"Fixed Variable," Hauser & Wirth, New York, NY

2013
"Art at the Core," Hudson Valley Center for Contemporary Art, Peekskill, NY
"The Cat Show," Curated by Rhonda Lieberman, White Columns, New York, NY
"Transmissions," Altman Siegel, San Francisco, CA
"Tenth Anniversary Show," Wallspace, New York, NY
"Yes I Will Yes," American Contemporary, New York, NY
"It's Over There," Matt Keegan and James Richards, Marie Lund, Rose Marcus, Emily Mast, Lucy Skaer, Viola Yesiltac, Simon Subal Gallery, New York, NY

2012
"Books," Matt Keegan, Adam Pendleton, Ricardo Valentim, Galeria Pedro Cera, Lisbon, Portugal
"Why Do Birds Suddenly Appear," Matt Keegan and Dane Mitchell, Zak Kitnick, Matt Sheridan Smith, Josh Tonsfeldt, Curated by Matt Moravec and Kyle Thurman, Volker Bradtke, Dusseldorf, Germany
"Yeah We Friends and Shit," Josée Bienvenu Gallery, New York, NY
"Found in Translation," Curated by Nat Troutman, Deutsche Guggenheim, Berlin, Germany

2011
"Circulate," Curated by Lauren Cornell, Fotografie Museum, Amsterdam, The Netherlands
"Short Stories," Curated by Isla Leaver-Yap, Sculpture Center, Long Island City, NY
"Exposure: Matt Keegan, Katie Paterson, Heather Rasmussen," Art Institute of Chicago, Chicago, IL

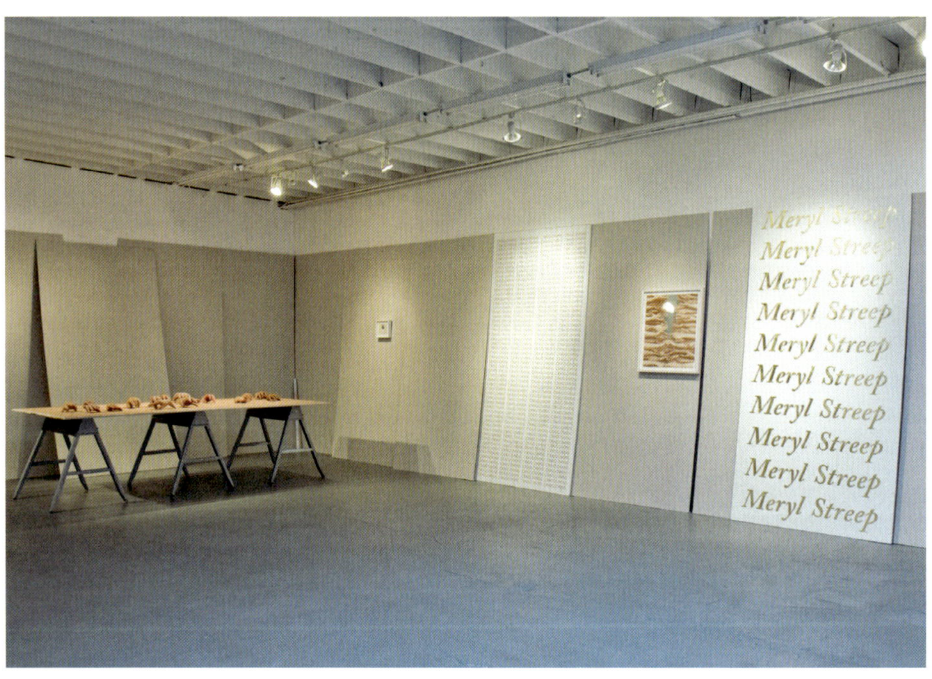

Installation View, 2008. "Now's the Time," Anna Helwing Gallery, Los Angeles, CA.

"The Air We Breathe," Curated by Apsara DiQunizio, San Francisco Museum of Modern Art, San Francisco, CA
"The Anxiety of Photography," Curated by Matthew Thompson, Aspen Art Museum, Aspen, CO
"We Are Grammar," Curated by Dave Beech and Paul O'Neill, Pratt Manhattan Gallery, New York, NY
"No More Presence," Hunter College / The Artist's Institute, New York, NY

2010
"Haunted: Contemporary Photography/Video/Performance," Guggenheim Museum Bilbao, Bilbao, Spain
"Image Transfer," Henry Art Gallery, University of Washington, Seattle, WA
"Held Up By Columns," Renwick Gallery, New York, NY
"Christmas in July," Yvon Lambert, New York, NY
"The Summer Bazaar," Tanya Banakdar Gallery, New York, NY
"…And Then There Was X," Altman Siegel, San Francisco, CA
"So Be It: Interventions in Printed Matter," Andrew Roth, New York, NY
"American Spirit," Crone Galerie, Berlin, Germany
"\ (Lean)," Nicole Klagsbrun Gallery, New York, NY
"Contemplating the Void: Interventions in the Guggenheim Museum," Solomon R. Guggenheim Museum, New York, NY

2009
"Younger than Jesus," New Museum, New York, NY
"Reach of Realism," MOCA Miami, Miami, FL
"Interim in Three Rounds," Curated by Jason Murison, Friedrich Petzel, New York, NY
"Picturing the Studio," School of the Art Institute Chicago, Chicago, IL
"Phot(o)bjects," Curated by Bob Nickas, Presentation House, Vancouver, Canada
"A Wild Night and a New Road," Altman Siegel, San Francisco, CA
"Separate Entities," Museum 52, New York, NY
"The Garden of Forking Paths," Maisterravalbuena, Madrid, Spain

2008
"Optimism," Westport Art Center, Westport, CT
"Democracy in America: The National Campaign," Organized by Creative Time, New York, NY
"Communication Breakdown," Andrew Edlin Gallery, New York, NY and Galerie Impaire, Paris, France
"Catawampus (for H.D.)," Midway Contemporary Art, Minneapolis, MN
"Intimacy," Curated by Anne Pasternak, The Fireplace Project, East Hampton, NY
"Imaginary Thing," Curated by Peter Eleey, Aspen Art Museum, Aspen, CO
"Rental," Curated by Haley Mellin, New York, NY
"Not so subtle subtitle," Curated by Matthew Brannon, Casey Kaplan, New York, NY
"11 Sessions," Orchard, New York, NY with Karin Schneider and John Miller
"Pawnshop," Organized by e-flux, New York, NY, travels to Museum Boijmans Van Beuningen Rotterdam, Rotterdam, The Netherlands and Beijing, China

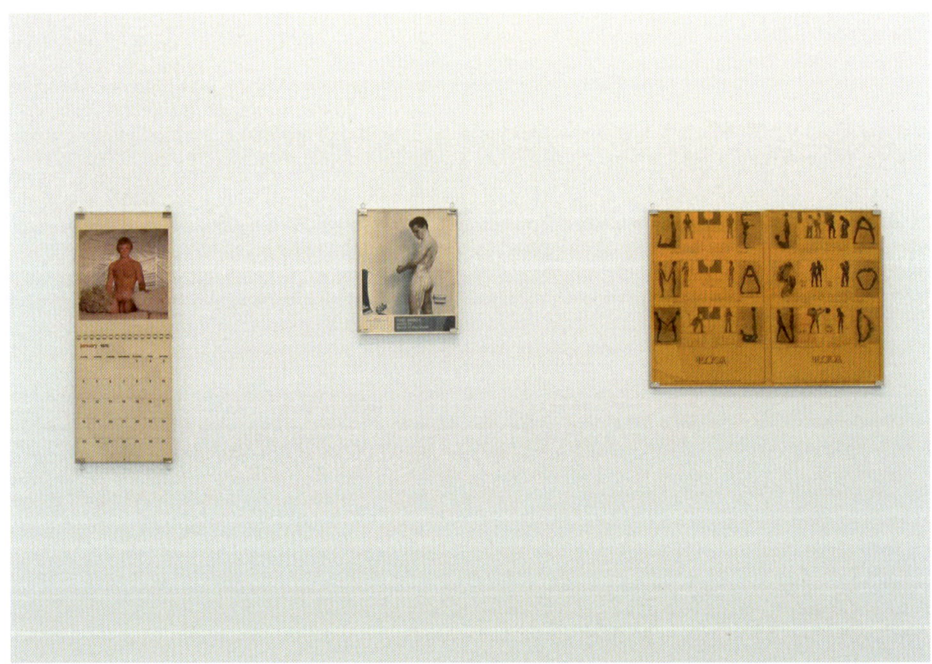

Calendars loaned from the The Gay, Lesbian, Bisexual, Transgender Historical Society, San Francisco, included in "Postcards and Calendars," 2009. Altman Siegel Gallery, San Francisco, CA.

2007

"I AM Eyebeam," Curated by Melanie Schiff and Lorelei Stewart, Gallery 400, University of Illinois at Chicago, Chicago, IL

"Catawampus (for H.D.)," Shane Campbell Gallery, Oak Park, IL

"NeoIntegrity," Curated by Keith Mayerson, Derek Eller Gallery, New York, NY

"Funny Shadows" with Daphne Fitzpatrick, Matt Keegan, Adam Putnam, and Allison Smith, Curated by Dinaburg Arts, Clifford Chance US, New York, NY

"Elastic Paintings and Transparent Partition: An exhibition by Karin Schneider, Forde, L'Usine, Geneva, Switzerland," Curated by Sarina Basta Alabama, in collaboration with Leslie Hewitt, Office Baroque Gallery, Antwerp, Belgium

2006

"Please Love Me," Curated by Santiago Cucullu and Nicholas Frank, Walker's Point Center for the Arts, Milwaukee, WI

"How I Finally Accepted Fate," Curated by Jason Murison, EFA Gallery, New York, NY

"Bring the War Home," Elizabeth Dee Gallery, New York, NY and QED, Los Angeles, CA

"A Rabbit as King of the Ghosts," Mitchell-Innes & Nash, New York, NY

"Mystic River," SouthFirst:ART, Brooklyn, NY, travels to: Arcadia University Art Gallery, Glenside, PA

"Supports," Roger Bjorkholmen Galleri, Stockholm, Sweden

Curatorial

2006

"Bunch Alliance and Dissolve," initiated and arranged by Public-Holiday Projects, Contemporary Arts Center, Cincinnati, OH

Artists Writings and Projects

2015

"==#2." Edited by Matt Keegan. New York: Capricious Publishing, January 2015.

2014

"Matt Keegan and Kay Rosen." *BOMB* (Summer 2014): 44–49

2013

"Playing House," *Texte Zur Kunst* (March 2013): 80–89.

Keegan, Matt. "The State of the Union." Presentation at CCS Bard, Annandale-on-Hudson, NY, March 4, 2013.

2012

"==." Edited by Matt Keegan. Paris: mfc michèle didier, 2012.

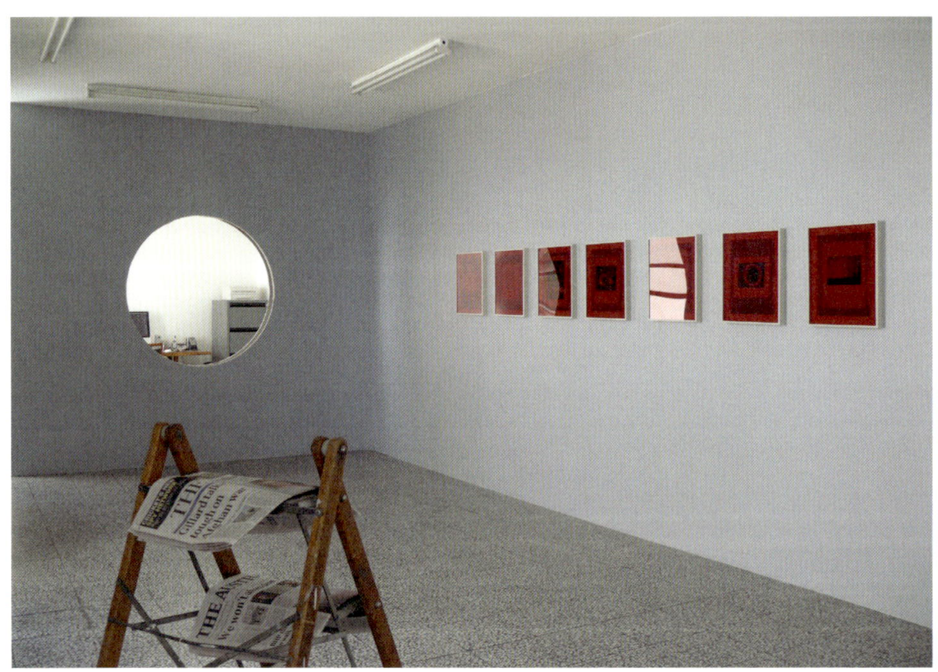

Installation view, 2010. "The Story of a Window (with Dane Mitchell)," Neon Parc, Melbourne, Australia.

2010

"Lost in Translation: Do you see what I read?." MAP – Journeys in Contemporary Art 24 (Winter 2010): 46–49.

"Haim Steinbach." *Mousse* 24 (Summer 2010): 82–87.

"North Drive Press Archive." SPACE: Library, London, UK, May 2010.

"Public Image Limited." *Artforum* (January 2010): 156–163.

2009

"We're Not There" with Jessica Dickinson. James Fuentes, New York, NY, August 2009.

2008

Keegan, Matt. "Members of the Same Symbiotaxium, but Probably Not Collaborators." By Fia Backström.

X-TRA 10, No. 4 (Summer 2008): 20–31.

Presentation for SkowheganTALKS at P.S.1 Contemporary Art Center, New York, NY, April 5, 2008.

2007

"The 'Urge' in Surge: Kay Rosen and Shannon Ebner Want to Have a Word with You." Art on Paper (July/Aug. 2007): 24–25.

"Straight to the Moon, Alice." *Modern Painters* (February, 2007): 84–89.

Keegan, Matt. "Artists at Work: Matt Keegan." By Audrey Chan. Afterall Journal (February 6, 2007).

2006

"Matt Keegan: Top Ten." *Artforum* (Feb. 2006): 98.

Public Collections

Alfond Collection of Contemporary Art at Rollins College, Winter Park, FL
Annette and Peter Nobel Collection, Zurich, Switzerland
Metropolitan Museum of Art, New York, NY
Solomon R. Guggenheim Museum, New York, NY
Whitney Museum of American Art, New York, NY

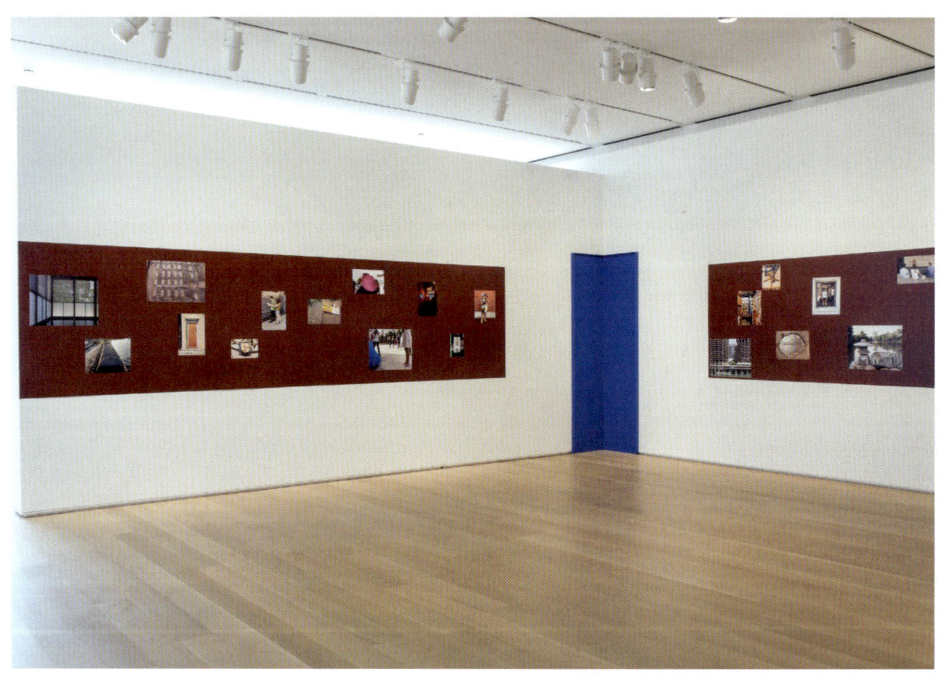

Installation view, September 3, 2011–March 4, 2012. "Exposure: Matt Keegan, Katie Paterson, Heather Rasmussen," The Art Institute of Chicago, Chicago, IL.

BIBLIOGRAPHY

2015

Cotton, Charlotte. *Photography is Magic*. New York: *Aperture*, Sept. 2015.

Kourlas, Gia. "Review: Joshua Beamish Takes On Challenges Within Couples, in 4 Takes." *New York Times*, Aug. 6, 2015.

"Over & Under." *New Yorker*, July 27, 2015.

Gabrielsen, Stian. "Pappfantomer." *Kunstkritikk*, Apr. 15, 2015.

Keegan, Matt. *Contemporary Art Stavanger*. Interview by Marte Danielsen Jølbo.

Westin, Monica. "Critic's Pick: Matt Keegan, And." *Artforum*, Feb. 5, 2015.

2014

Russeth, Andrew. "Matt Keegan and Anne Truitt at Andrea Rosen." *Artnews*, Dec. 2014, 112.

Kelsey, Colleen. "Matt Keegan: Form and Function." *Interview*, Sept. 11, 2014.

Fulford, Jason and Gregory Halpern, eds. *The Photographer's Playbook*. New York: Aperture, June 2014.

Keegan, Matt and Kay Rosen. "BOMB Specific." *BOMB*, Summer 2014.

2013

Alfond Collection. Art for Rollins, *The Alfond Collection of Contemporary Art, Volume I*, Edited by Abigail Ross Goodman. Winter Park: Cornell Fine Arts Museum, Rollins College, 2013.

Wilson, Eric. "Retailing as a Forum for Art." *New York Times*, Sept. 4, 2013.

Smith, Roberta. "Ten Years." *New York Times*, July, 25, 2013.

"Horizon." *Expresso, Atual*, May 18, 2013.

2012

Kitnick, Zak. "Federal Blue and Deep Cool Red: A Conversation with Matt Keegan." *Idiom*, Nov. 26, 2012.

Haraldseth, Geir. "My Apple." *Acne Paper*, Winter 2012.

Keegan, Matt. *Kaleidoscope*. Interview by Frank Benson, Fall 2012.

"Yeah We Friends and Shit." *New Yorker*, Aug. 13, 2012.

Pollack, Barbara. "Copy Rights." *Artnews*, Mar. 2012.

2011

The Air We Breathe: Artists and Poets Reflect on Marriage Equality, Edited by Apsara DiQuinzio. San Francisco: Museum of Modern Art with Distributed Art Publishers, 2011.

Fulford, Jason. "A History of New York." *IANN* 7 (2011): 101–116.

Wilson, Michael. "Matt Keegan, D'Amelio Terras." *Artforum*, Sept. 2011.

Fry, Naomi. "Frieze Focus: Matt Keegan." *Frieze Magazine*, May 2011.

Tagliafierro, Marco. "Critic's Picks." *Artforum*, Feb. 2011.

Asfour, Nana. "The Art of Giving." *Paris Review*, Jan. 27, 2011.

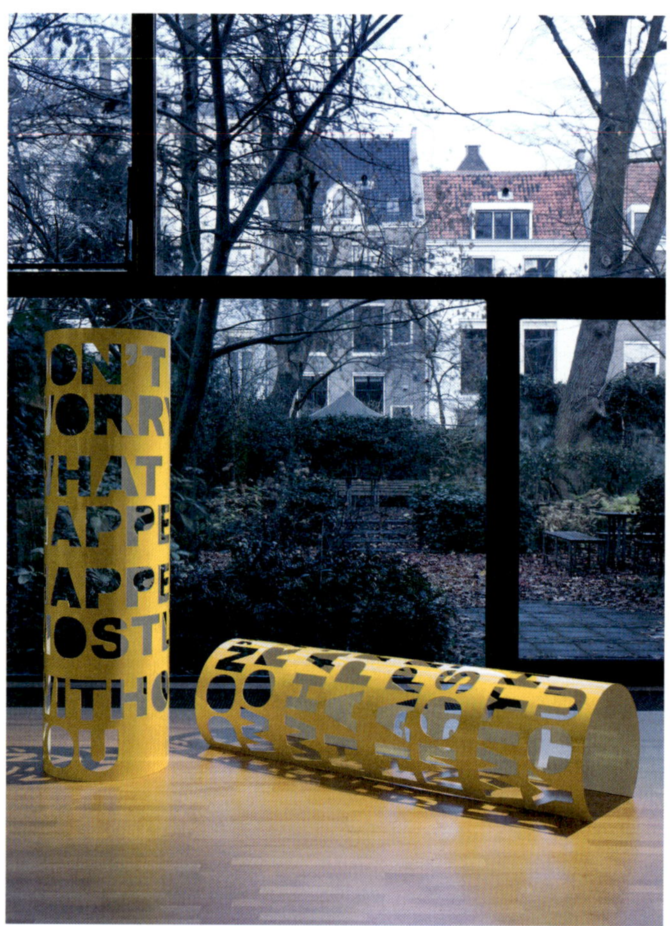

Don't Worry, A sculpture by Matt Keegan, from a poster by James Richards, of a poem by Josef Albers. Laser-cut and spray-finished steel featured in "Circulate," FOAM, Amsterdam, The Netherlands.

2010

Rule, Dan. "Around The Galleries: 'Matt Keegan & Dane Mitchell: The Story of a Window'." *Age*, Nov. 6, 2010.

The Studio Reader: On the Space of Artists. Edited by Mary Jane Jacob and Michelle Grabner. Chicago: School of the Art Institute of Chicago, June 2010.

Dot Dot Dot 20 (Summer 2010): 90.

Lay Flat: Meta 2 (Feb. 2010): 86.

2009

Vilas, Amber. "2009 in Review: Gallery Exhibitions." *artinfo.com*, Dec. 29, 2009.

"Alex Gartenfeld Discusses when Matt Keegan takes a portrait." *The Kingsboro Press* (2009): 49–52.

Words Without Pictures. Edited by Alex Klein. Los Angeles: Wallis Annenberg Photography Deptarment, Los Angeles County Museum of Art, 2009.

Craven, Ann. "Straight to the Moon, Alice! Straight to the Moon!" In *Ann Craven: Shadows Moon and Abstract Lies*, edited by Florence Derieux and Amy Granat, 35–37. Zurich: JRP | Ringier, Aug. 2009.

Huston, Johnny Ray. "Shades of Time: Q&A with Matt Keegan." *Pixel Vision* (San Francisco, CA), May 7, 2009.

Huston, Johnny Ray. "Matt Keegan gives form to his and SF's past in 'Postcards & Calendars'." *San Francisco Bay Guardian*, May 6, 2009.

Bibeau, Petra Royale. "'Time/Travel' Matt Keegan Postcards & Calendars (Altman Siegel)." *Artslant*, Apr. 27, 2009.

Killian, Kevin. "Generations." *Open Space*, April 25, 2009.

Cotter, Holland. "Young Artists Caught in the Act." *New York Times*, Apr. 9, 2009.

Miller, John. "Fun Gallery." *Grey Room 35* (Apr. 2009): 92–99.

Cashdan, Marina. "The Chosen Ones." *Manhattan Magazine*, Mar./Apr. 2009.

Dougles, Sarah. "Matt Keegan in New York." *artinfo.com*, Mar. 6, 2009.

Helfand, Glen. "Critic's Picks." *Artforum*, Feb. 2009.

2008

Olson, Marisa. "Keeping Hope Alive." *Rhizome*, Oct.14, 2008.

Ayeroff, Anna. "Matt Keegan at Anne Helwing." *Artslant*, Sept. 7, 2008.

Momin, Shamim M.. "Future Greats: Matt Keegan." *ArtReview*, March 2008.

2007

Banai, Nuit. "Matt Keegan." *Modern Painters*, Dec./Jan. 2007.

Shirreff, Erin. "Matt Keegan." *Art Papers*, Nov./Dec. 2007.

Grabner, Michelle. "I Am Eyebeam." *Artforum*, Nov. 2007.

Huberman, Anthony. *Afterall 16*, Autumn/Winter 2007.

"Goings On About Town: Matt Keegan." *New Yorker*, Sept. 24.

Knight, Nicholas. "Matt Keegan: Any Day Now at D'Amelio Terras." *Nicholas Knight* (blog), Sept. 7, 2007.

Smith, Roberta. "Art in Review, Matt Keegan & Jedediah Caesar." *New York Times*, Sept. 7, 2007.

Bentley, Kyle. "Associative property." *Artforum*. Feb. 1, 2007.

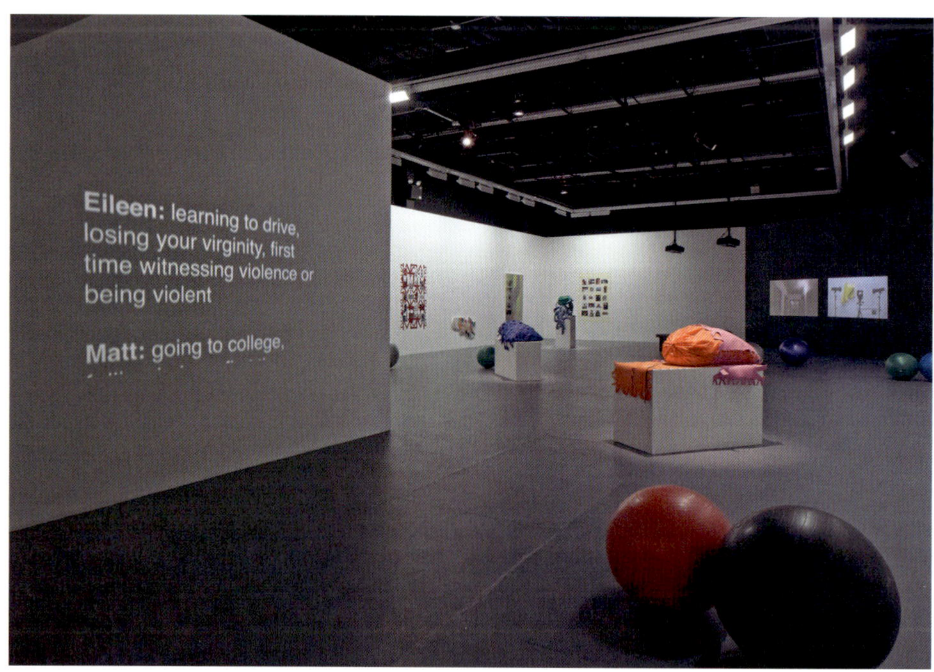

Installation view, 2012. "Y?O!G...A. (with Eileen Quinlan)," The Kitchen, New York, NY.

2006
Higgs, Matthew. "On the Ground, New York." *Artforum*, Dec. 2006.
Higgs, Matthew and Ralph Rugoff. "New York vs. London." *Modern Painters*, Sept. 2006.
Who Cares. New York: Creative Time Books, 2006.
Pollack, Barbara. "Bring the War Home." *Time Out New York*, Aug. 3–9, 2006.
Fry, Naomi. "A Rabbit as King of the Ghosts." *Artforum*, June/July 2006.
Schwendener, Martha. "Leslie Hewitt and Matt Keegan." *Time Out New York*, June 29–July 5, 2006.
Bryan-Wilson, Julia. "Repetition and Difference." *Artforum*, Summer 2006.
Alemani, Cecilia. "Mystic River." *Artforum*, May/June 2006.
Smith, Roberta. "Who Needs a White Cube These Days?." *New York Times*, Jan. 14, 2006.
Scott, Andrea K.. "The Best and Worst of 2005." *Time Out New York*, Dec. 29, 2005–Jan. 4, 2006.

ACKNOWLEDGMENTS

Thank you to Torunn Larsen and Hansi Hammonds for their work on "Portable Document Format" and special thanks to Geir Haraldseth for making that exhibition and this publication happen. Thank you to the Norwegian Arts Council for their funding, and to Altman Siegel & Galeria Pedro Cera for their generous support.

Thank you to Uri Aran, Anna Craycroft, Leslie Hewitt, Tom McDonough, John Miller, Jim Richards, and Sara VanDerBeek for their friendship and contributions to this book. To Nicole Lanctot for copyediting and Abraham Adams proofreading their writing. Virginia Overton and The Felix Gonzalez-Torres Foundation for contributing images to Tom McDonough's essay. Nicole Belangeil Kaack for her assistance in putting this publication together. Adam Michaels for co-publishing this book with Inventory Press, and to Shannon Harvey for her assistance. Special thank-yous to Rachel Hudson and Joseph Logan for their care, patience, time, and work on designing *OR*.

Looking back, I want to thank Shelley and Phil Aarons, Claudia Altman-Siegel, Luca Balser, John Bartolo & Chris Kinsler at Axelle Fine Arts, Mike Bratteli at Wicked Powder, Lance Brewer, Katherine Brinson, Helena and Ana Cardoso, Pedro Cera, Milano Chow, Chris D'Amelio, Luther Davis, Bridget Donahue, Doug Eklund, Dan Fox, Trina Gordon, Ann Greene Kelly, Vitória Guerra, Nathan Hauenstein, Matthew Higgs, David Kiehl, Belinda Kielland, Haruo Kimura at East Frames, Paul Kirschner at Enterprise Metalworks, Matthew Lyons, Sam Merians at Big Prints, Josh Minkus, Sophie Moerner, Cory Nomura, Julie & Murphy at Pochron Studios, Ann Schaffer, Daelyn Short Farnham, Jeremy Steinke, Andy Stillpass, Lucien Terras, Melissa Timarchi, Nat Trotman, Rachel Uffner, to my friends, with special thanks to Su Barber for her friendship and a decade of collaboration, Rich Aldrich, Fia Backström, Frank Benson, Matt Connors, Lauren Cornell, Jessica Dickinson, Matthew Dipple, Rachel Foullon & Ian Cooper, Sara Greenberger Rafferty, Stuart Kochmer, Isla Leaver-Yap, Lizzy Lee, Sean & Amy Lyons, Lisa Oppenheim, Eileen Quinlan, Jory Rabinowitz, Kay Rosen, Aura Rosenberg, Natalia & Enrique Sacasa, Molly Smith, Ryan Sullivan & Jeremy Rossman, Ricky Swallow & Lesley Vance, Lisa Tan, and Matt Wolf, and my family, especially my siblings, Jeanne, Denise, and Eddie, and mother and father for letting me include them in my work. And an *extra* special thank-you to Alex Gartenfeld.

—Matt Keegan

PHOTOGRAPHY CREDITS

"Portable Document Format," Rogaland Kunstsenter: Hans Edward Hammonds "And,“ Altman Siegel: Wilfred J. Jones; "Matt Keegan and Anne Truitt," Andrea Rosen: Lance Brewer; "Horizon," Pedro Cera: Bruno Lopes; "Y?O!G…A.," The Kitchen: Jeffrey Sturges; "Lengua," Altman Siegel: Wilfred J. Jones; "I Apple NY," D'Amelio Terras: Jason Mandella; "Exposure," Art Inst. of Chicago: Photography © The Art Institute of Chicago; "Found in Translation," Deutsche Gugg: Mathias Schormann; "Image Transfer," Henry Art Gallery: Richard Nicol; "New Windows," D'Amelio Terras: Adam Reich; "Postcards & Calendars," Altman Siegel: David Berezin; "Now's the Time," Anna Helwing: Brian Forrest

Opening images: 1–5: "Portable Document Format" at Rogaland Kunstsenter, Stavanger, Norway, 2015; 6–9: "And" at Altman Siegel Gallery, San Francisco, CA, 2015; 10–13: "Matt Keegan and Anne Truitt" at Andrea Rosen Gallery 2, New York, 2014; 14–17: "Horizon" at Galeria Pedro Cera, Lisbon, Portugal, 2013; 18–21: "I Apple NY" at D'Amelio Terras, New York, NY 2011; 22–25: "Lengua" at Altman Siegel Gallery, San Francisco, CA, 2011; 26–27: "Image Transfer" at Henry Art Gallery, Seattle. Wa, 2010; 28–29: "New Windows" at D'Amelio Terras, New York, NY 2009; 30–31: "The Generational Triennial: Younger than Jesus," at the New Museum, New York, NY 2008

Page 124: *OR (Positive)*, 2006 Sheetrock. Variable Dimensions. Photo credit: Jean Vong.

Matt Keegan: OR is co-published by

Inventory Press, LLC
167 Bowery, 3rd floor
New York, NY 10002
inventorypress.com

and

Rogaland Kunstsenter
Nytorget 17
4013 Stavanger, Norway
rogalandkunstsenter.no

This publication is a companion to Matt Keegan's exhibition "Portable Document Format," Rogaland Kunstsenter, March 14–June 7, 2015.

Edited by Nicole Lanctot
Designed by Joseph Logan and Rachel Hudson

Printed and bound in Belgium by die Keure

ISBN: 978-1-941753-10-1

Distributed in North America by
RAM Publications
2525 Michigan Avenue,
Bldg. #A2
Santa Monica, CA 90404
rampub.com

Distributed in Europe by:
Anagram Books
anagrambooks.com
contact@anagrambooks.com

This catalogue was produced with generous support from

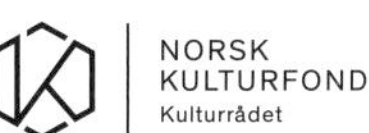

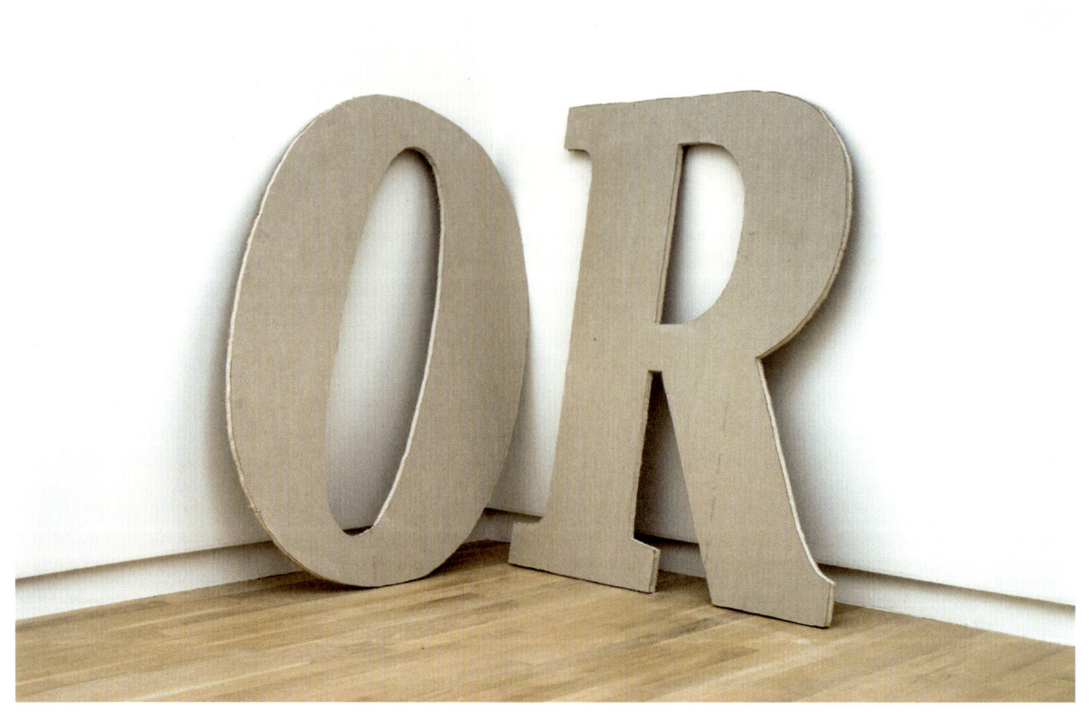
OR